# A HISTORY OF DOG SLEDDING IN NEW ENGLAND

# A History of Dog Sledding in New England

Bruce D. Heald, PhD

The History Press

Published by The History Press
Charleston, SC 29403
www.historypress.net

Copyright © 2011 by Bruce D. Heald, PhD
All rights reserved
*Front cover:* Winter Carnival in Berlin, New Hampshire, 1922.
*Photo by the White Mountain National Forest.*

First published 2011

Manufactured in the United States

ISBN 978.1.60949.264.9

Library of Congress Cataloging-in-Publication Data

Heald, Bruce D., 1935-
A history of dog sledding in New England / Bruce D. Heald.
p. cm.
Includes index.
ISBN 978-1-60949-264-9
1. Sled dog racing--New England--History. 2. Dogsledding--New England--History. 3. Mushers--New England--Biography. I. Title.
SF440.15.H435 2011
798.8'30974--dc23
2011019689

*Notice*: The information in this book is true and complete to the best of our knowledge. It is offered without guarantee on the part of the author or The History Press. The author and The History Press disclaim all liability in connection with the use of this book.

All rights reserved. No part of this book may be reproduced or transmitted in any form whatsoever without prior written permission from the publisher except in the case of brief quotations embodied in critical articles and reviews.

*This book is respectfully dedicated to those drivers and supporters who wish to preserve the legacy and heritage of the sport of sled dog racing in New England.*

# Contents

| | |
|---|---|
| Foreword, by Cynthia Molburg | 9 |
| Acknowledgements | 11 |
| | |
| I. THE BEGINNING | 13 |
| Early History of the New England Sled Dog Club | 13 |
| The Importance of Sled Dogs | 17 |
| Preparing a Team | 17 |
| The Junior Driver | 19 |
| Junior Mushers of Laconia | 20 |
| The Town Team | 23 |
| Sled Dog Driving | 26 |
| | |
| II. RACES AND EVENTS | 29 |
| Along the New England Trail | 30 |
| Sled Dog Schedules, 1929 | 32 |
| Point-to-Point Race | 34 |
| The Annual World Championship Sled Dog Race | 36 |
| Sled Dog Elimination Race for the 1932 Olympics at Wonalancet, New Hampshire | 40 |
| Sled Dog Olympics at Lake Placid, New York, 1932 | 41 |

# Contents

III. Introducing Famous Drivers — 43
Dr. Charles Belford, Claude Bellerive, Jean Boissonneault, Jean Bryar, Keith Bryar II, Keith Bryar Sr., Florence M. Clark, Dr. Roland Lombard, John Lyman, Jim Lyman, Emile Martel "Ole Fox," Deborah Molburg, Richard (Dick) Molburg, Ed Moody, Dick Moulton, Elizabeth Ricker, Eva "Short" Seeley, Leonhard Seppala, Emile St. Godard and Arthur Walden

Racing Sled Dog Champions — 80
Lady Mushers of the Past — 83

IV. Chinook — 85
Breeding — 86
"Short" Seeley and the Chinook Dog — 87
Chinook and Arthur Walden, "The Driver and His Dog" — 89

V. The Sled Dog — 99
Would You Like to Race a Dog Team? — 100
Spectator Tips — 100
The Sled Dog Racing Breeds and Musher's Vocabulary — 101
A History of Sled Dog Breeds — 105
Dog Team Members — 109
Sled Dog Racing—An International Sport — 111
From Nome to Candle — 112
The Famous Iditarod Trail — 113
Sled Dog Trails — 115

Index — 121
About the Author — 125

# FOREWORD

There was very little awareness of the hardy animals that provided the means of travel in the snow-covered, isolated regions of the world until the turn of the twentieth century, when the written material was made available to readers living in the more populated regions of the world. It appeared in books, both biographical and fictional, and in news releases related to the Arctic and Antarctic explorers of the time and the celebrated 1925 serum run to Nome by sled dog teams to save the far north Alaskan city from a potential diphtheria epidemic.

The first documented sled dog race to receive recognition outside the native villages in Alaska was the 1908 All Alaska Sweepstakes race from Nome to Candle and back, a distance of 408 miles. Then, and until the mid-1900s, men dominated the field of competitors, and "sprint" races involving ten- to twenty-mile heats held on weekends became most popular, especially in New Hampshire, the home of the famous three-day World Championship Sled Dog Derby in Laconia.

The inaugural 1973 race on part of the same trail used in the 1925 serum run heralded the return of interest in long-distance races. It was followed by the annual one-thousand-mile Iditarod Trail Race from Anchorage to Nome and over the years has encouraged challengers from throughout the world. The Iditarod, like no other race, has resulted in a new awareness of the sport and with it a need for more information about the dogs and what drives both men and women to devote years behind a dog team, often under the most demanding winter weather and trail conditions.

# Foreword

Dr. Bruce Heald's *A History of Dog Sledding in New England* is an earnest endeavor to cover myriad areas not generally included in a single book about sled dogs—their drivers, their heritage, their training and all that contributes to their performance as working and racing team dogs—and to bring readers up through the years into today's world of sled dog racing.

Dedicated racing fans will appreciate the more detailed accounts of the New England champions, including the emergence of talented female drivers, and those of the less celebrated people who have had an impact on the sport through their individual activities. The peripheral fan will gain information that will make attendance at sled dog races more enjoyable because of deeper appreciation of both the dogs and their drivers. And for those just looking for a "good story," there are several of them in the following pages.

Cynthia Molburg
Publisher, *Team & Trail*

# ACKNOWLEDGEMENTS

I would like to extend my appreciation to the following people and organizations for their assistance in creating this anthology of articles in order to preserve the legacy and heritage of the sled dog sport: Mildred Beach, Omer Berube, the Book Moose, Charles Booth, Jean Bryar, Keith Bryar II, Keith Bryar Sr., Jeffrey Bragg, the *Carroll Country Independent*, Maureen Clark, Clark's Trading Post, Nancy Cowen, Victor J. DiSanto, Terry Fifield, Mat Glover, Richard C. Greenwood, Jonathan Hayes, Roger Heath, the *Laconia Evening Citizen*, the Lakes Region Sled Dog Club, John Little, Douglas Heald, Cynthia Molburg, Deborah Molburg, Richard Molburg, Jim Miller, Paula K. Miner, Gail Ober, Bernice Perry, Leslie Pocock, the Poland Spring Kennel, the Ralston Purina Company, Elizabeth M. Ricker, Folgren Stevens, the Lyman family, *Team & Trail*, Victory Lane Photo, Arthur Walden, the White Mountain National Forest and Wikipedia.

# I
# THE BEGINNING

### EARLY HISTORY OF THE NEW ENGLAND SLED DOG CLUB

The first race in the East started at Berlin, New Hampshire, in 1922. It was a three-day race of 123 miles and was won by Arthur T. Walden in fifteen hours, thirty-six minutes, with Jean Label coming in second in sixteen hours, twenty-two minutes. The following year, the race was transferred to Quebec City on account of the wider scope afforded by that location and more general interest. The first of these races was run over a course of 131 miles; it was won by Jean Label in fifteen hours, fifty-five minutes, with Henry Skeen in second place in sixteen hours, thirty-five minutes. The New England Point-to-Point Derby was established in 1926 over a course of 140 miles, starting and finishing at North Conway, New Hampshire. The first derby was won by Shorty Russick in fourteen hours, thirty-one minutes, with Emile St. Godard coming in second in fourteen hours, forty-seven minutes.

In the year 1924, sled dog racing was officially recognized when the New England Sled Dog Club was organized in Wonalancet, New Hampshire, at the Wonalancet farm home of Mr. and Mrs. Arthur Walden.

Walden was a man interested in adventure in the outdoors. When the opportunity arose for him to acquire some dogs that seemed to adapt themselves to the dog sled, he started breeding for a team. He organized a club for dog racing in New England, and ever since then, the sport has flourished. Teams from Alaska, the Midwest, Canada and California, as well

# A History of Dog Sledding in New England

Arthur Walden of Wonalancet, New Hampshire—winner of the International 120-Mile Dog Race—is seen crossing the finish on the Androscoggin River in Berlin, New Hampshire.

as New England, have participated in the Laconia World Championship Sled Dog Derby.

During the early 1920s, the Brown Paper Company in Berlin, New Hampshire, organized an international race to be held near the border of Canada, an event that attracted much notice in the Boston and New York newspapers. Two Canadian and two American teams entered the race. The race was a three-day event, averaging thirty miles a day. Arthur Walden, with his lead dog, Chinook, driving a single hitch of nine dogs, won the race. The publicity spread nationwide, and Walden and Chinook became famous overnight.

It was at this time that enthusiastic fans of Arthur and Chinook gathered at the Wonalancet farm to establish a club in order to promote this new sport of sled dog racing. The club became known as the New England Sled Dog Club. The constitution and bylaws were adopted on November 5, 1924. Arthur Walden was chosen as its first president. Dr. Harry Souther of Boston, Charles DeForest of New Haven, Everett Rutter of Derry Village, Percy Estes of Meredith, Styles Oxford of Maine and Dustin White of Vermont were selected as vice-presidents in order that the entire New England area would have representation in the new organization. The first secretary-treasurer was Claude Calvert of Meredith, New Hampshire. Dr. Souther was appointed to the position of chief judge. The first official

# The Beginning

Clark's Eskimo dog team, West Milan, New Hampshire.

meeting was held at the office of Walter Channing in Boston. According to a report in the *Boston Transcript*, there were sixty charter members. At this time, it was decided to move the headquarters of the club from Manchester, New Hampshire, to Meredith.

In the winter of 1925, the newly formed club sponsored two races for "green dogs and green drivers." The races were held in Newport and Meredith, New Hampshire. The drivers were Hi Mason, winner of the Newport race; Walter Channing, winner of the Meredith race; Caryl Peobody; Mrs. Fred Lovejoy from Massachusetts; Percival Estes driving the Meredith team; Richard Stearns; and Clara Enebuske, later known as Mrs. Richard Read of Wonalancet, New Hampshire. Florence Clark of North Woodstock would have raced with her team of Eskimo dogs, but she did not qualify as a "green driver."

In 1926, there was a race held in Poland Spring, Maine, won by Arthur Walden. In second place was Walter Channing, and in third place was Edward Clark. The following year, at Poland Spring, Maine, Leonhard Seppala, hero of the serum drive to Nome, Alaska, won the race with a team of Siberian huskies. In that era of racing, big dogs were considered to be superior racers.

During the years from 1926 to 1928, point-to-point races were held in which teams started in one town, drove to another town, started there on the second day and drove to a third town to finish the race. These races attracted quite a few Canadian teams, and competition was keen. In 1926, the race ran from North Conway to Wolfeboro on the first day. The second day's finish was at Ashland, and racers finally returned to North Conway for the completion of the race. The competitors were: William Grayson, Joe Dupuis, Ed Clark, Shorty Russick, Arthur Walden, Walter Channing, Ed Brydges, Henri Skeen, Emile St. Godard, Francois Dupuis and Phillip Molley. First prize was $1,000—Shorty Russick was the winner. The three-day mileage was about 140.

According to the Thompson-Ames Society's "Historical Highlights," written for the *Gilford Streamer* in February 2005, the first race recorded in the Laconia region was between a team owned by Charles Lyman and a team from Meredith in 1926 as part of the Laconia Winter Carnival. Charles Lyman became known as "Laconia's Mr. Sled Dog."

In 1927, the race ran from Wolfeboro to Ashland on the first day, from Ashland to North Conway on the second day and from North Conway to Wolfeboro on the third and final day, for a total of 135 miles. The winner that year was Leonhard Seppala, and the first prize was again $1,000. Other entrants were: Emile St. Godard, Theodore Kingeak, Hiram Mason, Walter Channing, Arthur Walden, Victor Lavigne, Francois Dupuis, Joe Dupuis and Phillip Molley.

In 1928, over the same course, the contestants were: Hiram Mason, Mrs. E.P. Ricker, Emile St. Godard, Walter Channing, Ed Clark, Ed Bridges, Leonhard Seppala and Shorty Russick. The prize money was $1,000 for first place; $500 for second place; $300 for third place; $200 for fourth place; and $100 for fifth place.

At this time, Arthur Walden and Chinook went with Admiral Byrd to the South Pole on the first Antarctic Expedition. During Walden's absence, the club began to deteriorate. Mr. and Mrs. Milton Seeley took over the operation of the Chinook Kennels and the Wonalancet farm. Walter Channing, a member of the original organization, urged the Seeleys to reorganize the club and start it rolling again. Races were held in various New England towns each winter until U.S. involvement in World War II and gas-rationing restrictions brought racing to a standstill.

Many owners of Siberian huskies either sold or donated their dogs to the Air Sea Rescue unit of the army for the war effort, where under the direction of Colonel Norman Vaughan and other service personnel—namely William Shearer III, William Belletete and Tate Duval, to mention a few—the dogs were trained to rescue the crews of downed aircraft in Greenland, Baffin

# The Beginning

Island and other northern areas. Some dogs were shipped to Europe with the idea that they could help evacuate the wounded from the Battle of the Bulge. This never became necessary.

From 1927, the New England Sled Dog Club again resumed its racing schedule, with six to ten teams competing each weekend during the winter months. Since that time, the sport has grown by leaps and bounds, with an increased number of both junior drivers and senior drivers, including a five-dog open class and an amateur class.

It looks as if the sled dog sport is here to stay. The greatest hazard it faces is the lack of good snow for the teams.

## THE IMPORTANCE OF SLED DOGS

It is important to remember that sled dogs enabled men and women to venture into frozen land, which would be inaccessible by any other means. These dogs, capable of pulling tremendous loads—and going for days with little food—first opened the way to the gold fields of Alaska, made it possible to reach the North and South Poles and were integral in the success of the Byrd Antarctic Expeditions.

Before the advent of the modern airplane, sled dogs were the only means of freighting supplies and necessities in the North. Even today, weather conditions must be favorable before planes can take off, while sled dogs trot on and on under the worst imaginable conditions.

## PREPARING A TEAM

*Dick Molburg, manager of the* Team & Trail *publication and a respected sled dog trainer and breeder, wrote and contributed this article on how to prepare a winning team for a championship race.*

The process of training a dog team for a championship race actually starts years in advance of the event with the selection of puppies, usually from known stock. These pups, at seven or eight months of age, will commence to undergo a rigorous conditioning and training program, lasting over a period of nearly two years, to attain the proficiency needed for the most demanding races.

Usually, the dogs that run on the top performing teams in the racing classics will have had at least one year, and very possibly several years, of experience in less demanding events before their mettle is tested in international competition.

Once the basic members of the team have been selected as the result of the observations of the trainer in preliminary trials, the actual training process for the big February World Championship Derby begins. Shortly after Labor Day, as soon as the first cool day of fall arrives, the team is hooked to a "gig," which could vary from a three-wheeled motorcycle-type vehicle to a small car with its motor removed. Training at this time is generally limited to exercise-type runs to start building up the basic muscle structure of the animals, which had been relatively inactive during the hot summer months.

By mid-October, the basic unit should be shaping up to the extent that the driver has some idea of which dogs in the selected group are likely to "make" the team that will enter the big race, still some months away.

As the days grow cooler in late fall, the distance covered by the team is usually on backcountry dirt roads. If the proper terrain and road surface are available, the dogs will cover up to ten miles in a single run several times a week. Since sled dogs would rather run on snow than dirt, the arrival of the first snow is welcomed by sled dog drivers, and the serious training commences.

Training runs become more frequent, and distances are lengthened gradually to meet the number of miles that will be asked of the team on the actual race trails; a few somewhat longer runs are thrown in to test the basic ability of each member of the team to stand the rigors of racing against the best in sledding competition, sometimes in weather conditions calling for added endurance.

As the physical demands of training increase, greater attention is given to the nutritional needs of the sled dogs. Their basic rations are supplemented with increasing amounts of fat for energy and meat to ensure an adequate supply of high-quality protein for proper muscle development.

Most often, shortly after the first year, the teams will be entered in several races, allowing them to continue their basic training and also test the performance of the dogs as a unit in actual racing conditions.

Like the human athlete, the sled dog team has a training schedule that is geared for peak performance in the major event of the season. Although serious training continues throughout the actual racing season, time is allotted for necessary breaks to rest the team members and to maintain the continuing desire to run at their best when the big challenges confront them.

Then, one morning, the racers and the teams are at the Laconia starting line. Over the next three days, and after fifty-four miles, the drivers will know

# The Beginning

if their years of planning and the five long months both the driver and the dogs have invested in concentrated training will lead them to that victory for which they are aiming.

## THE JUNIOR DRIVER

*Many years ago, Ms. Paula K. Miner wrote a brief story about the junior driver. The following excerpts are from this article.*

> *Any youngster, regardless of the gender, but loves dogs may qualify as a Junior Driver. They must be willing to clean, feed and train their dogs. The New England Junior Sled Dog Club was established with these objectives in mind.*
>
> *...The strict rules by which the young people must abide are similar to the rules set up by the adult drivers. These racing rules bring out the quality of good sportsmanship, responsibility and a respect for both dogs and drivers on the trail.*
>
> *...The junior drivers are made up of two classifications. Youngsters from the age of five to the age of twelve run over the course of approximately one*

Competition is close here in the Junior 10-Mile dog sled race. This is one of the most interesting winter sports in New Hampshire.

# A History of Dog Sledding in New England

You're never too young!

mile with one dog hitched to their sled. This encourages a child to acquire stamina, co-ordination, and the ability to cope with both the dog and sled when faced with a problem with the dog, or an obstacle on the course. It also fosters resourcefulness and a healthy sense of competition. When this skill is accomplished, the junior driver may move up to the two- or three-dog class, and compete on a course of five miles. The approval for this advancement is given by the chief judge, only when he feels that the driver is ready to handle his or her team under different weather conditions and trails. A junior driver may remain in the two- or three-dog class until he or she is sixteen, although some experienced juniors may move up before this age and are accepted by the senior club and its drivers.

...Competition in the junior sled dog club is divided evenly between the gender. Many young ladies wish to show that this sport is where the gender is no barrier. No concessions are asked and none are given.

## JUNIOR MUSHERS OF LACONIA

*Omar Berude, a great musher in his own right, has contributed this brief story of "The Kids and Their Dogs."*

# The Beginning

Steve Giguere is seen racing his three-dog team in the junior races in Laconia.

Sled dog racing, like baseball, has its little league. It is a sport where "a kid and his dog" become one against the world. Quite often, a youngster would see a sled dog race and then go home and hitch his family pet to a sled. That's how it all began.

At the first race, the dogs ran, crawled or were dragged over the one-hundred-yard course to the hilarious delight of the crowd, while the moms and dads whistled and pleaded with their canines to cross the finish line. Obviously, there was more spirit than class, but it was the beginning of a series of World Championship Junior Races in Laconia, New Hampshire.

Gradually, the young "mushers" began to produce remarkably well-trained dogs and thus became more competitive. The program grew until 1969, when it reached its zenith with 113 entries in the one-dog and three-dog races.

The first sled dog races to be held in Laconia, New Hampshire, took place in 1929 and 1930 as part of a series of weekend events in the Northeastern states sponsored by the New England Sled Dog Club. In 1931, the Laconia Sled Dog Club was formed by some prominent citizens in the city, and future "Lake City" races were locally promoted.

# A History of Dog Sledding in New England

This three-dog junior team of Irish setters races along the Laconia Trail.

The "World Championship" title was adopted in 1936, and races were held annually until 1938, when they abruptly ended. With the advent of World War II, many of those who participated in the races were pressed into military service.

It wasn't until 1956 that sled dog racing returned to Laconia. In that year, a two-day February weekend was sponsored by the Belknap County Sportsmen Club, and in 1957, the former members of the Laconia Sled Dog Club banded together to create the Lakes Region Sled Dog Club for the purpose of producing the World Championship Derby.

During those years of sled dog racing, competition was limited to adult drivers, and Ed Benoit, with Hector "Pete" Sevigny and fellow members of the city's VFW Post 1670, decided to do something about it. They organized the first World Championship Junior Sled Dog Derby, and the youngsters from throughout the Lakes Region were at the 1957 starting line with their talented and not-so-talented sled dogs spanning a variety of breeds, including Siberian huskies, French poodles, St. Bernards, beagles and just plain old family mutts.

## The Beginning

At about the same time, adult one-dog, three-dog and five-dog racing classes gained recognition and popularity, causing the number of children racing small teams to decline. In the late 1980s, the well of junior mushers was drying up, and it was hard to produce a good field of drivers. Junior contests were dropped from the Laconia racing schedule.

In 1988, with the encouragement of Omar Berube and the support of the VFW Post 1670 members, the World Championship Junior Sled Dog races were put back on the schedule, and in 1989, twenty youngsters in the one-dog and three-dog classes participated in the races.

Just as Little League has been a springboard for Major League Baseball, junior sled dog racing has become a significant source of adult racers. Some of the most respected drivers started as juniors. Even for those who don't make it to the "pros," there are great rewards for participating in junior sled dog racing. The youngsters gain self-assurance, not only in handling dogs but also in handling themselves.

During all that time, the VFW Post 1670 never lost sight of its commitment to junior mushers, and the "Kid & Mutt" races continue for local youngsters.

## THE TOWN TEAM

### *Meredith, New Hampshire*

In the early 1920s, Arthur Walden and his Chinook dog started the sled dog sport in New Hampshire. Meredith at that time was a "going town." Two men, Claude Calvert (town clerk) and Sam Hayward (reporter) were pushed to get Meredith on the map. They enjoyed getting things going and into the greater Boston papers. Meredith had its Old Home Days, a two-day—sometimes three-day—event. The whole town became involved, so what better place to start a Winter Carnival?

The carnival started with Arthur Walden exhibiting his team and giving short rides on Meredith Bay. The people who worked on the carnival were Judge Small, Charlie Cowing, Percy Estes, Clarence Calvert and Sam Hayward. These gentlemen organized the carnival and saw to it that there was something going on every minute—ski jumping, skating races, snowshoe trips, hot oyster stew and sleigh rides. Through it all, Arthur Walden and his team were busy giving spectators rides on the bay.

Out of this, interest in a dog team for the town of Meredith developed. A group of men—namely H.B. Rust, owner of Meredith Electric (later

# A History of Dog Sledding in New England

Ed Gordon and the Meredith Town Team on Meredith Bay, 1930s.

known as the White Mountain Power Company, now the New Hampshire Cooperative); Phil Bacon, owner of a restaurant and livery stable, who had his fingers in all the pies to further the development and tourism in Meredith; Claude Calvert, town clerk, who loved to organize any activity for the town; Charlie Cowing, owner of a neighborhood grocery store; and Percy Estes, a mechanic at Pynn's Garage who had many years of experience with dogs—got together and bought some dogs from a gentleman by the name of MacMillan in Maine. The dogs were brought to the Lakes Region.

The team was to be known as the Meredith Town Team. Percy Estes and Charlie Cowing were to take care of the housing and feeding of the dogs. Percy was to drive, with Charlie as his helper. The dogs were kept in Cowing's barn and outside pens across the street from Bacon's Restaurant (about where Bay Point Inn is presently located).

The leaders of the town team were Ipa and Nachussets; their four puppies (Chipala, Okala, Ipungo and Metic) made up the rest of the team. They were hitched one behind the other. The team did quite well. They were a big hit with spectators at all of the out-of-town races.

At that time, there were no vehicles with cage boxes for the dogs to be transported out of town. If the train schedule was right, the dogs (all loose),

# The Beginning

sled, harnesses and both drivers could be put in the baggage car and went as far as possible. When the end was reached, the dogs and their gear were unloaded and hitched up, food and extra clothing were piled in the sled and the team drove the rest of the way to the racing site, be it five or fifty miles. To get to Newport from Meredith, the team was transported by train to Concord, and the dogs drove the rest of the way to Newport.

Florence and Ed Clark from North Woodstock drove all the way to Meredith, Newport and Maine with both their little boys in the sled.

During the early days of sled dog racing, the drivers had no trails, so they made them as they traveled to the races. Of course, the teams were made up of what we presently know as freight dogs, and the sleds were not much better; some were practically made of two-by-fours.

Over the years, the Meredith team owners felt that perhaps a new leader would improve the speed of the team, so they eventually purchased a new leader from Mrs. H. Lauderdale of Blackfoot, Idaho. Wolf, the new leader, arrived with a letter telling what commands to use and which explained his disposition, habits and tricks. He worked out very well with the team. However, he was kept at Charlie Cowing's place, where a little white dog was also housed. The two canines became best friends. It seems that Charlie went on a weeklong hunting trip and took his dog. Wolf missed his new pal; he laid around and refused to eat. On the night before Charlie's return, Wolf jumped through a very high and small window in the barn. The next morning, he was found dead, hanged by the neck. His toenails had scratched up the ground, and he had torn two boards off the building, but because of his disposition, he had been unable to bark. Wolf was greatly missed.

During the early days of the first dog races, Percy Estes and Charles Cowing continued to develop the town team. Eventually, Meredith produced more teams, the largest of which was Ed Gordon's. These dogs had black and white markings, while the town team was white with black heads and patches. Ed always used red pompoms on the harness. Ed's new team gained more speed, but they were pretty, and they served an important role in the sled dog history as they were exercised, fed and trained by Dick (Pooch) Moulton. Dick was a skilled and talented trainer and driver; he was never seen without a dog. Lots of Meredith children got into dog racing by helping with the town team or those of Ed Gordon, Bill Pynn Marden, Dick Moulton, Bob Prescott and Charlie Roberts. All had small teams of their own.

Many of the New England Sled Dog Club meetings were held in the meeting room over Bacon's Restaurant in Meredith. Florence Clark and Short Seeley, newcomers to the club, became an asset to the promotion of the sport. Added to the list of early drivers were John Davidson, Roger Haines, Dick Moulton, Bill Marden and Almon Ricker.

Through the interest and special efforts of the early drivers of the town team, a new sport was born in New Hampshire and the country.

## Sled Dog Driving

*Mrs. Elizabeth M. Ricker, an early participant in the New England Sled Dog Club and an authority on sled dog driving, provided the following article on sled dog driving during the formation of the club in 1929.*

It is unfortunate that many writers about the North Country delight in branding the husky as a fierce "man-eating" brute, ready to tear his master limb from limb. These writers have given a false impression that the dog team has become synonymous with cruel and abusive treatment. It appears that they have been made to believe that the husky is practically a wild animal and is held in submission only by the terror of the sting of his driver's lash.

It has taken time to overcome this prejudice; however, it has been accomplished largely through the dog races, where it has been shown that the winner is the driver who has used care with his or her dogs and driven the race not with the whip, but with the head. If a driver has resorted to the lash in order to gain speed, it is plain to detect it in the attitude of the team, and a good driver knows that if a dog lacks ambition, it can never be beaten into him—he grows worse if anything, for when robbed of his enthusiasm he is thoroughly useless.

A dog and his team will respond readily to his driver. If a dog has a driver who is constantly finding fault, he eventually grows tired of hearing the incessant nagging and ceases to pay attention to it. The secret lies in making the dogs realize that when the driver speaks, he means it. It would be easier to convince the skeptical "un-believers" if they could stand somewhere along the snow-covered trail and see a team swinging along together rhythmically, the driver standing on the runners of the sled, his voice breaking the stillness of the sharp winter's morning in a lilting folk song, ballad or just whistling a tune while the dogs lope along as if they understand his carefree holiday mood. They are carefree, too, for they know that their driver is pleased.

What is essential and foremost in dog racing is the control and the laborious training, the skillful mastery in the handling of the team and the endless patience of treating the dogs as individuals.

# The Beginning

The training and discipline are most crucial in driving open and even limited teams; especially, open sixteen or eighteen dogs are common now.

[*Note*: The limited-class race consists of a team of six dogs, which is run over a shortened trail, typically about 60 percent the length of the open-class event. The open class, alternately called the unlimited class, is not limited in the number of dogs in a team. There may be as many as twenty dogs pulling a line, which requires a tremendous amount of training.]

It is hard to believe that in this age of science and speed, we have borrowed from the aborigines the simple mode of travel and organized dog races. In so doing, we are actually protecting the sled dog and giving him a chance, for in spite of our current mode of transportation, there are still places where the dog team is the sole means of transportation, and through the sled dog races his living and driving conditions will be improved. In the United States, racing is a comparatively new sport.

Hence, the birth and development of the sled dog races should be considered a boon in humanizing the treatment of the sled dog. It is not only the welfare of the dog during the race that counts, but it is [also] in the race that the care of the months previous manifests itself.

The races will eventually prove the advantage of the animal with coat and feet suited to the rigors of the trail. They will show the dogs that may cover the ground in the shortest time and arrive at their destination in the best condition. But, above all, possibly the finest thing the races will demonstrate is the necessity for unity and partnership [that] must exist between dogs and driver.

# II
# RACES AND EVENTS

Sled dog racing involves the timed competition of teams of sled dogs that pull a sled with dog drivers or mushers standing on the runners of the sled.

A sled race was considered a demonstration sport at the 1932 Winter Olympics in Lake Placid, New York, an event that we will examine later in this chapter.

Sled dog races include the sprint races over short distances of four to twenty-five miles; the mid-distance races, which range from twenty-eight to two hundred miles; and the long-distance races of two hundred to possibly over one thousand miles. The sprint races are usually two- or three-day events, with runs on successive days with the same dogs in the race. Mid-distance races are either heat races of fourteen to eighty miles per day or a continuous race of over one hundred miles.

Races may be categorized not only by distance but also by maximum number of dogs allowed in each team. The most popular categories are the four-dog, six-dog, eight-dog, ten-dog and unlimited, which is referred to as the open class.

Most races are organized either as timed starts or mass starts. In the timed starts, teams start one after another in equal timed intervals, competing against the clock rather than against one another. In mass starts, all the dog teams start simultaneously. These races are very popular in foreign countries such as Canada and Europe.

In the United States and Canada, the ISDRA (International Sled Dog Racing Association) sanctions most races. For the race to be sanctioned, a

# A History of Dog Sledding in New England

Runner-up in the 120-Mile International Dog Race at the finish line, Androscoggin River, Berlin, New Hampshire, February 1922.

variety of rules must be adhered to. For example, the ISDRA sanctioning rules specify that all hazards should be avoided and that trail distances must be reported correctly and must be clearly described to the competitors. All drivers must treat their dogs humanely, and enhanced substance abuse is forbidden.

In this chapter, we will examine the 1929 sled dog racing schedule, the racing season, the longest race, the point-to-point race and, finally, the Annual New England Championship Sled Dog Derby in Laconia, New Hampshire. Later, in chapter four, we will examine the driver and his dog.

## Along the New England Trail

Even though dog teams were in wide use throughout parts of Canada and the northeastern United States, the New Hampshire activities were largely responsible for the great spread of the sport in New England. The Granite State ranks first in sled dog races, followed by Maine, Massachusetts and Vermont.

Early in New England races, point-to-point events were the order of the day. Usually, these were from one village to another around Lake Winnipesaukee's Lakes Region, which included such towns as Meredith, Laconia Center Harbor, Moultonborough, Ashland, Wolfeboro, Alton Bay, Tamworth, Sandwich and Wonalancet, to name a few.

# Races and Events

Included in the early New England Sled Dog Club races were those presented in Wonalancet. Tamworth was the traditional beginning of the New England racing season. This race offers one of the most scenic trails in the Lakes Region, located at the base of the famous Chocorua Mountain in the White Mountains. This particular event, even though it offered a small purse and some trophies, attracted drivers from all over the United States and Canada.

According to Cynthia Molburg, publisher of *Team & Trail*, the following observation was given during the 1960s:

> *Meredith has produced many first, second and third generation drivers... many of the original "Mushers" are now taking an active part in the official business end of the New England club. During its early years, Meredith sponsored and supported a "Town Team" as did many towns in the region, which competed in various races around the countryside. Percy Estes of Meredith was its first official driver. Though Meredith had abandoned the sport, it still retains many active drivers and interest in the sport.*
>
> *With the advent of well-plowed roads and faster travel, the New England Sled Dog Club has spread its racing activities to Vermont, Maine, Massachusetts and Canada; some Mushers even travel to Alaska.*
>
> *It was at Poland Springs, Maine, that Leonhard Seppala met Mrs. Peg Ricker, and with her formed the kennel from which the popularity of the racing Siberian huskies emanated. Many of the Siberians now running the New England trails can be traced back to this original kennel.*

Laconia, New Hampshire, the capital of sled dog racing in the Northeast, has been involved with the sport since 1922. The Laconia World Championship Sled Dog Derby, sponsored by the Lakes Region Sled Dog Club, is probably the largest race outside Alaska and is traditionally held during the first weekend in February.

Arthur Walden of Wonalancet offers an interesting account of how sled dogs came to New England:

> *Dog driving in New England began about 1921 with a team of half-bred St. Bernards. This team was used for pleasure almost entirely, although occasionally they did work that horses could not accomplish on account of the rough terrain of the country.*
>
> *This team, as far as we know, was the first belonging to New England. Occasionally a team from the Northwest had come in or one from an Arctic exploration. These were used for exhibition purposes.*

*The first New England team passes on the way of all dogs but was overlapped by puppies born of an Eskimo mother and a mongrel father, whose descendants have been seen at most of the large carnivals and races.*

*The fist time the husky appeared in public was at a carnival given by the Forest Service (White Mountain National Forest) at Gorham, and they created quite a stir in that area. The next year 1922 at the same carnival, here was the first official sled dog race in New England, a Canadian team against an American. There were only three dogs on a team and the race was only six miles from Berlin to Gorham, New Hampshire, and the American team was defeated. It was a poor race, but a starter for the sled dog sport.*

*W.R. Brown of Berlin got up the following year, a three-day race of 123 miles, and it was won by an American team. The next year the race went to Quebec, Canada, by default of American teams and has been run there for many years since.*

*People in general had the idea that dog driving was confined to racing, since a sport of any kind is first to break into sprints, but this is not so. The greatest pleasure is the driving. The whole northern New England lies open to the man who has a team of two dogs or more.*

The sport has gained a great deal of respect for both the driver and the spectator. Since its inception, sled dog racing draws hundreds to the seasonal races in New Hampshire.

## SLED DOG SCHEDULES, 1929

As we look over the old records of the Laconia club, we note interesting information dated December 10, 1929, regarding a new plan for the annual sled dog derby schedule in that city for February, announced after a meeting of local businessmen and officers of the New England Sled Dog Club. At the meeting in the chamber of commerce room, the change was suggested as an aid to create more interest in sled dog racing, which had grown by leaps and bounds since its inception a few years earlier. The suggestion was to change the contest from point-to-point to a unified affair outside of town.

Arthur D. O'Shea, a Laconia merchant, presided at the meeting. Among those present were Lawrence B. Holt, Mayor Charles J. Hayford, Dr. C.E. Rowe, Fred S. Roberts and Edgar B. Prescott.

Races and Events

The New England Sled Dog Club officers present included Moseley Taylor, president; Dr. Harry A. Souther, vice-president; Robert Davis, secretary-treasurer; and William McDonald.

The course was laid out for three days in February. The distance was about forty miles a day. The towns of Ashland, Wolfeboro and North Conway were eliminated. This race would be centered in Laconia, New Hampshire, and this would control the arrangements under the auspices of the New England Sled Dog Club. There was every prospect that unified direction would make the race the best ever held in this section of the country.

The route of the first day (February 11, 1929) would start in Laconia at the fairgrounds and would run to New Hampton, through Bristol Hill and back to Sanbornton Square and Laconia, a distance of more than thirty-nine miles. On the second day, the route would run from Laconia to Belmont through Stewart Corner, Canterbury, Northfield and, finally, back to Laconia. On the third day, the route would lead to Meredith Center, through Meredith Village to Center Harbor, across Lake Winnipesaukee to Bear Island, from the island to Glendale and home again to Laconia, a distance of thirty-eight miles.

## The Racing Season

The season's racing schedule for the 1929 winter began at Lake Placid, New York. The second race would be the invitational affair at Poland Spring, Maine, on January 25 and 26. Both Lake Placid and Poland Spring were short-distance races. The third event was the Laconia race. The fourth would come in Quebec, Canada, where the Eastern International was held about two weeks after the Laconia race. The fifth would be at the reinaugurated two-hundred-mile nonstop race at The Pas, Manitoba, Canada, where Leonhard Seppala was expected to compete with men like Emile St. Godard, Earle Brydges and Shorty Russick. St. Godard and Brydges were also expected to race at the Laconia race. The presence of St. Godard and Seppala would mean the third year of the fight to outdo each other.

## The Longest Race

The route of the longest sled dog race ever scheduled in New England—from Berlin, New Hampshire, to the Mechanics Building on Huntington Avenue in Boston, Massachusetts—was announced on January 10, 1929, by the management of the New England Sportsman's Show, which was sponsoring the race in cooperation with the Eskimo Dog Club of America.

A sport primarily of the North Country would be for the first time staged for the benefit of the thousands of Bostonians who had never been privileged to view the Eskimo dog sled team in action. A prize of $1,500 was posted by the management of the Sportsman's Club Show, who thought it would attract the entries of many of the top dog sled teams throughout New England.

The race started at Berlin, New Hampshire, on January 14 and finished at noon on January 19. The route was as follows:

Monday, January 14: Berlin to Littleton (forty-three miles) by way of Gorham, Jefferson, Twin Mountains and Bethlehem.
Tuesday, January 15: Littleton to Plymouth (forty-five miles) by way of Franconia Village, Franconia Notch, Flume, Lincoln, West Thornton and West Campton.
Wednesday, January 16: Plymouth to Franklin (more than thirty-one miles) by way of Bridgewater, Bristol and Hill.
Thursday, January 17: Franklin to Manchester (thirty-seven miles) by way of Boscawan, Penacook, Concord and Suncook.
Friday, January 18: Manchester to Lowell, Massachusetts (thirty-one miles) by way of Nashua, Massachusetts.
Saturday, January 19: Lowell to Boston (thirty miles); best snow route, if any, to be chosen to finish at the Mechanics Building in Boston.

## POINT-TO-POINT RACE

### *North Conway–Laconia Race*

Another interesting account from the club's early records, dated February 1929, of a race from North Conway to Laconia, New Hampshire, indicates the following:

> *Sled dogs of eight teams yelped and pulled at the traces in North Conway this February morning, eager for action as the annual three-day point-to-point race of the New England Sled Dog Club got under way.*
>
> *A three-inch snowfall covered a solid inch foundation, but the roads, in fair condition, made further postponement unnecessary. The race originally had been scheduled to start a day before, but conditions did not allow it.*

# Races and Events

Winter sport at the carnival in Conway, New Hampshire, February 1922.

*Hi Mason of Tamworth was the first to get away promptly at 10:00 am for the first day's fifty-seven mile run through Center Harbor and Meredith to Laconia, NH. The first plans to lay the route over the ice on Lake Winnipesaukee from Center Harbor to Laconia were changed when it was learned that there was insufficient snow on the lake.*

*Mrs. E.P. Ricker of Poland Spring, Maine, set her dogs in motion five minutes after Mason. Then, at five minute intervals, starting in the following order were some of the biggest names in sled dog racing: Emile St. Godard of The Pas, Manitoba, Canada; Walter Channing of Boston, Massachusetts; Edward P. Clark of West Milan; Earl Brydges of The Pas, Manitoba, Canada; Leonhard Seppala of Alaska; and Shorty Russick of The Pas, Manitoba, Canada.*

*The drivers agreed that the morning's temperature of 21-degrees was a little higher than they would have liked. Ten degrees colder would have made it better for the dogs, they said.*

*Sunday was a day of rest, and the final run back to North Conway was scheduled for Monday. The total distance for the three days was about one hundred and thirty miles.*

*The race was for a cash prize of $2,300. The winner would receive $1,000 and the driver whose dogs were in the best condition at the end of the race would receive a special prize of $200.*

According to the *Laconia Evening Citizen* of February 1929:

> *The Laconia people were on their tiptoes awaiting the arrival of the dogs from North Conway. All day a large crowd watched the progress of the teams as indicated by the huge bulletin board in the window of the Laconia National Bank, these reports furnished by the central New Hampshire Telephone Company.*

Leonhard Seppala made the best time over the first nineteen miles from North Conway to Laconia. At the nineteenth mile point on a steep hill, three miles north of Tamworth, his elapsed time was one hour and forty-two minutes.

Earl Brydges was a close second, at one hour and forty-six minutes, followed by Emile St. Godard, one hour and forty-eight minutes; Hi Mason, one hour and fifty-seven minutes; Mrs. E.P. Ricker Jr., two hours and five minutes; and Walter Channing, two hours and fourteen minutes. Shorty Russick and Ed Clark had not reached that point when the times of the others were taken.

Leonhard Seppala received first prize in the derby from Mayor Harford. Seppala's dogs earned him the $1,200 and a $200 award for the best-conditioned dogs in the race. St. Godard received $500; Mason won $300.

## THE ANNUAL WORLD CHAMPIONSHIP SLED DOG RACE

### *February 1929*

The following account was originally printed in the *Laconia Evening Citizen* in February 1929:

> *The big day is here. Laconia has turned itself over to the dogs. The canines, pure-bred and mongrel bred in New Hampshire, Canada and Alaska are gathered here for the Annual New England Sled Dog Championship Race.*
>
> *Fifteen teams are quartered in different parts of the city, and the sharp yelping of the dogs has become music to the ears of the residents who are worked-up to a high pitch of enthusiasm over the three day race which gets underway at 10 o'clock tomorrow morning and sends six teams on the start of 126 miles, forty miles of which will be run tomorrow and the remainder on Tuesday and Wednesday, February 12$^{th}$ and 13$^{th}$.*

# Races and Events

A leaping leader is anxious to get started in this world championship race in Laconia. This team is using a "double lead" setup.

*Although the balmy weather of the past few days has melted much of the snow, an inspection trip today revealed that there was plenty of snow on the route for the first day's race and the committee in charge announced tonight that everything will go off as scheduled.*

*The route for all three days covers forty-three miles, starting and ending in Laconia, New Hampshire.*

*The first leg of the race takes the drivers from Laconia to Meredith Center, then to New Hampton and on through Bristol to Hill, across through Sanbornton Square to Lockmere and then back to Laconia over Lake Winnisquam.*

*A second race of two days for drivers not experienced enough to compete against veteran mushers from the United States, Canada as well as Alaska will be held over a thirty mile course Tuesday and Wednesday, while the major derby is going on. There is a great deal of interest in the smaller race because most of the entries are from New Hampshire. Ike Legasse of Littleton and Harold Pendergast of North Conway, both well known here, will fight it out in the race for the fourth* time this winter. Lagasse, presently a resident of Littleton and driving for the outing club of that town, is a native of Laconia.

While the drivers in the circuit will come for their share of attention, the greater interest is devoted to the "Clover leaf" event, which carries the New Hampshire title as the reward of victory, and the $1,000 first prize money.

Leonhard Seppala of Alaska, who won fame when he rushed serum to Nome, and now driving for the Ricker-Siberian Kennels of Poland Springs, Maine, and Emile St. Godard, youth veteran of the trails of La Pas, Manitoba, will test strength again over a long route.

Pre-derby predictions are that Seppala and St. Godard will fight it out for first place this year. The Alaskan has won the International race for the past two years, but last winter St. Godard turned around and defeated his rival in their second meeting of the season at La Pas. The rivalry between the Alaskan and the young, wiry, enthusiastic and popular Canadian is apparent in the excitement over the race.

New Hampshire has one driver by the name of "Hi" Mason of Tamworth, who is associated with Mosley Taylor of Boston in the Mason-Taylor Kennels. While several other drivers have gone hundreds of miles to muster a team of dogs, "Hi," a World War One veteran, has his homegrown team waiting for the gun to be fired by Dr. Harry A. Souther of Boston, one of the most familiar figures at the dog derbies. Mason is out to win better than third place, as he did two years ago, in the point-to-point race by showing as much speed as he did when driving a motorcycle over the roads of France during the war.

Mrs. Elizabeth P. Ricker Jr., of Poland Springs, Maine, now rated as a veteran, was present at the races bemoaning her fate that she could not drive a team over the long route, for while her team and that of Seppala were training at Lake Placid recently, they were in a collision with an automobile that injured some of the dogs and made it even doubtful if either driver could come to New Hampshire.

Seppala has merged the two teams together and now has a fast hitch of short-legged, high tensioned Siberians that have both speed and endurance. His closest rival, St. Godard has a team of long-legged dogs, a cross between Greyhounds and huskies, weighing about seventy-five pounds each, and working best under adverse conditions.

The husky wolfhound team, owned by Walter Channing of Boston, will be driven by Thomas Dadney and will mark the first time that the well known supporter of dog races will relinquish hold of the geepole in the race. He finished second to Seppala at Lake Placid this winter.

# Races and Events

*George Chevrette of Quebec will drive a team of husky-greyhounds for Scot Furrier of Boston and Hartford, Connecticut, while A. Carmac Marqueis, Ltd., of Quebec will have a team driven by Arthur LaPointe.*

*St. Godard is driving for the Iver Johnson Sporting Goods Company. Chevette is making his first appearance in the New England race, but four winters ago he finished second to St. Godard in the International Derby at Quebec.*

*Final preparations for the race were made via a committee meeting in the Chamber of Commerce room after the drivers and officials made a trip over the forty-mile course for tomorrow and reported plenty of snow on the route. This announcement dispelled any fear that the derby would not go through as planned, though if warm weather shows itself tomorrow, the route may be changed for the second and third days.*

*Tuesday's race will take the teams to Meredith Village, Center Harbor, Long Island Bridge, Governor's Island drawbridge via Daniel Webster Highway to The Weirs, to Lakeport via highway and Lake Paugus and to Laconia. On Wednesday, the teams will leave Laconia for Belmont, to Gilmanton, Gilmanton Ironworks, Alton, Alton Bay, West Alton, Glendale via Lake Winnipesaukee route, inside Moose, Rattlesnake and Diamond Islands to Lakeport and the grand finish in Laconia. Leonhard Seppala won the first place in the 1929 Sled Dog Championship Derby.*

## *Laconia World Championship Sled Dog Derby Past Race Results*

The following list contains the year and winner of each race.

| | |
|---|---|
| 1929 Leonhard Seppala | 1958 Art Allen |
| 1930 Emile St. Godard | 1959 Art Allen |
| 1931 Emile St. Godard | 1960 Keith Bryar |
| 1932 Leon Hamel | 1961 Ernie Brunet |
| 1933 Emile St. Godard | 1962 Keith Bryar |
| 1934 Roger Haines | 1963 Keith Bryar |
| 1935 Harry Wheeler | 1964 Dr. Charles Belford |
| 1936 Ovide Carrier | 1965 Dr. Charles Belford |
| 1937 Philia Daigle | 1966 Dr. Charles Belford |
| 1938 Harry Wheeler | 1967 Eddie Sylvain |
| 1939–1955 Races cease (World War II) | 1968 Dick Moulton |
| 1956 Dr. Charles Belford | 1969 John Piscopo |
| 1957 Emile Martel | 1970 John Piscopo |

1971 Dick Moulton
1972 Lloyd Slocum
1973 Dick Moulton
1974 Race cancelled
1975 Dick Moulton
1976 Dick Moulton
1977 Harris Dunlap
1978 Eugene Corbin
1979 Deborah Molburg
1980 Deborah Molburg
1981 Race cancelled
1982 Harris Dunlap
1983 Race cancelled
1984 Doug McRae
1985 Charles Erhart
1986 Race cancelled
1987 Gary Edinger
1988 Eddy Streeper
1989 Terry Killiam
1990 Don Beland
1991 Race cancelled

1992 Race cancelled
1993 Serge Pomerleau
1994 Don Beland
1995 John Samburgh
1996 Neal Johnson
1997 John Samburgh
1998 Race cancelled
1999 Eddy Streeper
2000 Real Turmel
2001 Neal Johnson
2002 Keith Bryar II
2003 "Buddy" Blayne Streeper
2004 Real Turmel
2005 Race cancelled
2006 Race cancelled
2007 Claude Bellerive
2008 Claude Bellerive
2009 Rudi Ropertz
2010 Race cancelled
2011 Keith Bryar II

## SLED DOG ELIMINATION RACE FOR THE 1932 OLYMPICS AT WONALANCET, NEW HAMPSHIRE

The following account appeared in the *Carroll County Independent* on January 22, 1932:

> *The New England Sled Dog Club has 20 entries for the Olympic Tryouts. All members of the New England Sled Dog Club were allowed to enter, but the rules stated that they must hold a record of a minimum elapsed time of two years standing in a three-day championship race; together with a 60% racing record annually.* Three judges with split second watches were appointed. The race of three days started from the Wonalancet farm over Lower Mountain Pass to McCrilles Trail to Whiteface Intervale, through Sandwich Covered Bridge onto Brown Circuit Road and return; a total of twenty-five miles.
>
> The first two placed were to enter the Olympics at Lake Placid in February, 1932. The Chinook Kennel Team #1 placed first in the tryout, and the Moseley Taylor #1 team placed second. With the permission of

Races and Events

*the Olympic Committee, Mrs. Milton Seeley, paying her own expenses, raced her malamute team in the Lake Placid Olympic Race.*

*The race took place February 6 and 7. Contestants started at three-minute intervals. The trail was 25.1 miles long. The governing bodies were the New England Sled Dog Club, Inc., (President—Moseley Taylor) and the demonstration Dog Derby Committee.*

## SLED DOG OLYMPICS AT LAKE PLACID, NEW YORK, 1932

A sled dog race was included as an exhibition sport for the only time at the 1932 Winter Olympics in Lake Placid. Five contestants from Canada and seven from the United States competed. The event, run under the rules of the New England Sled Dog Club, ran twice over a 25.1-mile course. St. Godard and Seppala would place first and second, with St. Godard taking first place after winning both the 50-mile races involved.

Victor J. DiSanto, PhD, gave an in-depth account of the 1932 Olympics in Lake Placid. This account was reprinted in *Adirondack Life* in January/February 2004. The excerpts in this section are from the early account.

*A group of champion mushers from Canada, New England, and Alaska gathered in Lake Placid, New York with their teams of Canadian Eskimo dogs, Alaskan malamutes, Siberian huskies, and Quebec Hounds for the third Olympic Winter Games.*

*Among the top contenders were three champions of sled dog racing: Canada's Emile St. Godard and Shorty Russick, and Alaskan Leonhard Seppala.*

*Drivers for the 1932 Olympic race—five Canadians and seven Americans—were chosen on the basis of earlier race results, with the New England Sled Dog Club races acting as qualifiers. The two most prominent Canadians, Russick and St. Godard, were seen training hard using the run-and-glide technique in order to lighten their load.*

The American racers included two veterans of Richard E. Byrd's first Antarctic expedition (1928–1930), Norman Vaughan and Roger Haines. Haines's team was owned by Moseley Taylor, president of the New England Sled Dog Club. In addition to the qualifying teams, there was a team of Alaskan malamutes owned by Eva Seeley of New Hampshire. Eva Seeley was the only woman to enter the race; she had won permission to participate from the Olympic committee.

The race was administered according to New England Sled Dog Club rules. Teams consisted of seven dogs: a lead dog plus six dogs harnessed in pairs. The contestants had to run a 25.1-mile course along roads and bridle paths on consecutive days; the total time for both runs would determine placement. Every dog in the race had to cross the finish line, either on its feet or in the sled's basket.

*The third Winter Olympiad had officially began on February 4; the race was held on Saturday and Sunday, February 6 and 7. On the day of the contest, spectators gathered at the start and lined the trail to watch and cheer. The loop course began at the Olympic Stadium, and made a circuit using Wilmington River, Cascade and Adirondak Loj Roads; then on trails to John Brown Farm State Historic Site and back to the stadium in the village.*

*The race began at 2:15 p.m., and as expected it became a duel between Seppla and St. Godard. During the first day of the race, one of Seppala's huskies could not continue and had to be hauled on the sled the last five miles. Yet the American champion finished the first heat less than ninety seconds behind the front-runner St. Godard. The Antarctic veteran Roger Haines collapsed from exhaustion at the finish, his strength drained from running up hills behind the sled.*

*The second heat began twenty-four hours after the first. Spectators lined the route once again, and at every point where the racers crossed the highways, crowds were so thick that the state troopers were needed to ensure the trail was clear.*

*St. Godard's team widened its lead on the second day, beating Seppala's team by more than seven minutes. St. Godard's Canadian hounds averaged more than 11.5 miles per hour for fifty miles. In a close race, St. Godard, Seppala and Shorty Rissick took gold, silver, and bronze respectively.*

## *The 1932 Olympics Demonstration Sled Dog Race Results*

| PLACE | DRIVER | TOTAL RACE TIME |
| --- | --- | --- |
| 1 | Emile St. Godard (CAN) | 4:23:12.5 |
| 2 | Leonhard Seppala (USA) | 4:31:01.8 |
| 3 | Shorty Russick (CAN) | 4:47:44.6 |
| 4 | Harry Wheeler (CAN) | 5:02:54.1 |
| 5 | Roger Haines (USA) | 5:06:27.3 |

# III
# INTRODUCING FAMOUS DRIVERS

This chapter is intended to introduce some of the pioneer sled dog drivers and their accomplishments, which characterize their excellence in the sport of dog racing. This brief representation by no means suggests that these are the only drivers worthy of mention, but it is a beginning in the annals of the great mushers who have shown exemplary achievements on the New England sled dog trails.

## Dr. Charles Belford

Dr. Charles Belford had been racing for over forty-five years. At the age of seventeen, he placed fifth in the Laconia World Championship Derby. At Ely, Minnesota, he placed fifth. He took third place at Bemidji, Minnesota, and fifth at Kalkaska, Michigan. In 1972, he came out of a six-year retirement.

His 1973 season saw him win eighth place at the All American Championship in Ely; eighth at Fairbanks, Alaska, in the North American Championship; and a big first place at Soldatna, Alaska.

Dr. Belford raised and trained his two hundred Alaskan dogs, which were housed at his Pocumtuck No. 2 Kennels in Deerfield, Massachusetts. Dr. Belford was known as a prominent veterinarian.

To list his World Championship accomplishments, we must include his first place finishes in 1956 at 3:07:35; in 1964 at 3:45:56; in 1965 at 3:38:05; and in 1966 at 3:56:57.

Dr. Belford was a master driver and a true asset to the sport of sled dog racing.

Dr. Charles Belford (#38) and his two lead dogs getting ready for the Laconia World Championship Race, 1966.

## CLAUDE BELLERIVE

According to Keith Bryar II, "Claude Bellerive had the best team seen on the Laconia Race. The sled-holders at the starting line could not hold the team, so the sled was four feet in the air." A credit to the sport, Claude won two World Championship races in Laconia: in 2007 at 2:11:25 and in 2008 at 2:27:39.

# Introducing Famous Drivers

## Jean Boissonneault

To profile Jean's racing experience, we would say that he is a master musher. Jean started racing at Laconia in 1975 with his father's dogs and never missed a Laconia race, except in 1985, when he won the Quebec City International Carnival Race and in 1999, when he raced in Fairbanks, Alaska (ONAC).

During Jean's career in the Laconia races, he took second place in 1980 and 1994. However, many times he won the Best Canadian Team in the open class, and he won the Omer Berube Memorial Trophy three times in the unlimited class. A highlight in his racing career was when he won the New England Sled Dog Club Unlimited Class (NESDC) in 2004, 2005, 2007 and 2008. He also won the Down East Sled Dog Club (DESDC) race in Maine several times in the unlimited class between the years 1995 and 2006.

In the international awards, he won the 2003 and 2006 Bronze Adult Sled Unlimited Medal.

Today, you may see Jean race in the Jackson, Maine Sprint Race; the Eden Mountain Sled Dog Race in Vermont; the Lakes Region World Championship Race in Laconia; the Northeast Championship Race in Jackman, Maine; and the Hill Village, New Hampshire Sled Dog Race.

## Jean Bryar

If you've ever met a champion, then surely you've met Jean Bryar. Besides her numerous accomplishments, she was a winner of the North American Women's Championship Sled Dog Races. She is no stranger to the sport.

Jean was born in New York City and first became interested in showing dogs in 1945 while living in Kansas. When she and her husband, Keith, moved to Massachusetts, they began to race, and in 1949, they entered their first competition. At this time, the Bryar-Patch Kennels became a reality, and in 1958 they moved to Center Harbor, New Hampshire, and established a reputation as one of the finest race teams in the Northeast. In 1967, the kennel became known as the Norvik Kennels.

Jean has been an active member of the Alaskan Musher's Association, the Lakes Region Sled Dog Club and the New England Sled Dog Club. Jean's active racing tours took her to St. Agathe and Quebec City, Alaska, and of course around the New England circuit. In addition, she has raced in New York, the Midwest, Manitoba and Ottawa.

The following is an interesting account of one of her races in Alaska:

# A History of Dog Sledding in New England

Jean Bryar is seen crossing the finish line in the Laconia World Championship Race.

> *Anchorage is a tough race and particularly tough for the native dogs because many of them are fairly wild and spooky when they come out of those villages, and when you pull them out of Fourth Avenue and through deep, deep crowds for probably twice the distance of Laconia's Main Street starting line, a lot of them shoot down those side streets and nobody can touch them; they will bolt. Your heart always bleeds for those boys who come in with those spooky leaders out of the bushes. What will spook the dog most is the sound and confusion of the crowd and its reflections of the city buildings.*

It is worthy to note that Jean Bryar was very influential in the training of nine World Championship dog teams. Today, Jean has retired in Florida but still continues to have a strong interest in the Lakes Region Sled Dog Club. She follows her son's accomplishments with great pride and enthusiasm.

## *Jean Bryar Tops in North American Classic*

Fairbanks, Alaska, April 7. Thousands of Alaskans, clad in fur parkas and mukluks stopped their shouting. There was a dramatic pause, and then the

# Introducing Famous Drivers

loudspeaker boomed: "Mrs. Jean Bryar of Center Harbor, New Hampshire, is the Women's Champion of the 1962 North American Sled Dog Derby."

Mrs. Bryar smiled; hundreds of cameras clicked. The champion responded, "This is the greatest thing that's ever happened to me in sled dog driving."

There was good reason for the New Hampshire woman to be smiling. She had done something no other woman outside Alaska had ever done. She had won the toughest sled dog race for women in the world.

This three-day race was held in Fairbanks, Alaska, the state's second-largest city, in connection with its Winter Carnival, and it drew visitors from all over Alaska and the lower states. In winning this race, Jean Bryar had matched the strength, skill and courage of both herself and her dog team against the rugged female Alaskan mushers. Most Eskimo and Indian dogs are considered some of the fastest Alaskan huskies.

In three days and thirty-four miles of racing over a firm Alaskan bush trail, Jean had posted the shortest total elapsed time of 135.50 minutes, only seven seconds ahead of Fairbanks's Rosmary Losensky.

The musher had come from behind to win the race because Fairbanks musher Janice Lundgren had won the first two heats and was thirty-nine seconds ahead of Jean in total elapsed time. On the third heat, the New England musher had the job of bettering the time of the Fairbanks musher, a favorite with the crowd.

Then the break came. Just as the Fairbanks musher was coming out of the starting chute, her team bunched up, and a coil of loose line got wrapped around the leg of one of the lead dogs. The dog, snapping to get free from the line, excited the other members of the team. Before Lundgren could do anything about it, a fight had developed.

By the time Ms. Lundgren had stopped the battle and straightened out the tangle of lines, she had lost about three minutes. Jean Bryar gave her dogs a hoot and surged around her rival.

About a minute and a half later, Ms. Lundgren repassed Jean, and the two staged a pass-and-repass duel over part of the trail. Mrs. Bryar settled down to trail Janice across the finish line.

Though Ms. Lundgren managed to make it up to the finish line ahead of Jean Bryar, she had lost too much time battling the tangle. The Fairbanks musher had to settle for third place in the overall standings.

Curiously enough, Jean won the championship without placing first in any heat. What is more important, she consistently placed high and posted the shortest total time in completing the three heats. The shortest total time is what counts, according to the rules, in winning the championship.

Ruth Bergman, who finished fourth, was one of the mushers who was stalled behind Ms. Lundgren's tangle. Despite the delay, she finished 42:12 on Friday and promptly improved her time to 39:43 on Saturday. Mrs. Bergman won Sunday's heat in 57:24. Many fans felt she might have had a good chance at first place had she not been delayed in Friday's race.

The trails were in good shape for Saturday's and Sunday's races, although the four-mile extension, which made the course into a fourteen-mile circuit on Sunday, was reported to be quite soft in spots.

"Sled dog racing in Alaska and in the eastern United States are two entirely different things," Jean Bryar said. She pointed out that Alaskan race trails are cut through the deep snow and are designed for speed.

"Up here, your courses are packed and cared for each week. This makes a big difference. We never run on the same track twice back home. Sand and salt raise additional difficulty," Jean added, "for as soon as there is a snow fall, the public works department is out with their sanders and salt, and that doesn't help our course a bit."

Not long ago the question was posed to her, "What preparation do you make for the race?" Jean replied:

> *The most important thing is that you have a gang of dogs to choose from. It is not the dogs you race, it's the dogs you don't race; the dogs you leave at home. The ability to know, before a race or that minute before the race, to look your team over and say, "Yah, that's OK, he'll go!"*

## KEITH BRYAR II

### *A Legend in His Own Time*

*When you've grown up in the shadow of New England mushing legends like MacDonald, Moulton, Molburg, Lombard as well as my parents, Jean and Keith Bryar Sr.—it does leave an impression.*
—*Keith Bryar II*

Keith was born in 1958 and went to a two-room schoolhouse in Center Harbor, New Hampshire. Both his mother and father were champion sled dog drivers. Keith was fourteen when he would go home after school and then go out training with a family friend, Alan Wiggin. He had a seven-dog team of Dobermans. Keith and Alan used to train on Squam Lake after

## Introducing Famous Drivers

Keith Bryar II is seen crossing the finish line with a clean sweep to capture first place in the World Championship Sled Dog Derby in Laconia, New Hampshire, February 2011.

school. Keith related that as he got older, he would train his mother's leftovers on the lake. Both his mother and father were very competitive people. They were hard-driven people. Like Dick Molburg said, "If those two had stayed together, kid, you'd be a multimillionaire now."

Keith reflects that his mother wanted to win the Women's Rondy race, and his father didn't want to give up the team for the North American the following weekend. "So, right from there you could see she wanted the best, too. My dad didn't want to see the best go out because he wanted to make sure they had a week's rest."

Greg Sellentin interviewed Keith for an article in *Mushing* magazine in January 2010. The following is excerpted from that conversation:

> *Q. So you had a family of sled dog stars.*
> *Keith: Yeah, I got a lot I try to live up to. My dad was a three-time winner of the World Championship Derby in Laconia. He also helped to keep the Laconia Club (Lakes Region Sled Dog Club) together. Between him and my step-dad, Dick Moulton, I remember them both telling me: "Never ever try to be president of the Laconia race!" It's one of those things I'll never forget.*
> *Q. When did you start going to sled dog races and trying to develop your own team.*
> *Keith: It was it 1985 when I got a couple of dogs from Tim Redington—That's how I started—very small. I was working with Dick Moulton. We'd get a large parcel to log and we'd work until 3:30, I'd have the dogs and get home around 7:00, in the house by 8:00 and then I'd do it all over again. It was fun back then because you didn't have the big number of dogs, only twelve. You had a lot of teams, but only a few great teams back then. They were always better in shorter races.*

For many years, Keith had successfully raced in Canada (the Quebec races) and in Alaskan races, as well as in the World Championship Sled Dog Derby in Laconia.

> *Q. It [the World Championship] was the biggest open-class race outside Alaska—you finally won that race in 2002. What can you tell me about it?*
> *Keith. This was my first World Championship victory in Laconia, and because of this it brought a lot of pressure off me. I had a lot of seconds and thirds at the race. In 2000 and 2001, I think Turmel and Neal beat us. Neal I know in 2001. I finally won it in 2002. We had a 56-minute run in 18 miles and then 57 and 58 three consecutive days. I tried to beat Neal the year prior and leased a few dogs from Turmel. I had a leader that couldn't get run up [by the point dogs] because if he did, he felt pressured. He'd turn around and get in a dog fight so of course the first day I didn't get 2 miles out of the starting line and I got a rip roaring dog fight going. He had a better team—he beat us.*

# Introducing Famous Drivers

*It was a relief off my shoulders. I hated getting insults by fellow drivers. "You'll never be as good a dog driver as your dad or your mom!" I said, "Yeah, you might be right." When I started, I started with a bunch of bums, well, not bums. If I had only started with Moulton's team. Maybe I would have changed the course of history.*

*He had a great team. It took me 10 to 15 years to get a team as good as what Moulton and my mother had when they finished. So it was a lot of pressure to get my first win. When we got a lot of top threes at Laconia and just one win. I hope this year we can...you know.*

*We screwed up last year. We ran real close to Rudi Ropertz, and I loaded a dog and was 40 seconds behind in the first day after loading and carrying a dog four miles. The second day I had a point dog that needed to be on the left and she was on the right and this dog would not run on the right. She crowded the dog so much they started to fight each other. We lost a terrible amount of time to Rudy. We slowly gained it all back through the race and probably put in the fastest time at the last third of the race because we lost so much. We screwed up. We could have ran within seconds of Rudi and might have been able to beat him but loading a dog and having a major shutdown the second day took us out of it. We were close to Rudi. He was a great gentleman, a great guy. He represented his country and the sport very well.*

*Today, I have one of my best teams ever; however, I don't see myself racing like Dick Moulton, until I'm 65 or whatever age, like Lombard. I see myself a little slower under those crunch situations: getting dogs re-hooked up. I'm not as fast as I used to be. I feel like 90% there. I'd like to be 15 years younger again. The plans are just to take it day-by-day. I'm looking and thinking about North, but it's a long time-frame from Anchorage until the rest of the races. I'd love to do village races. The big race I haven't raced yet now in Anchorage. I'd love to do it once in my career.*

During Sellentin's conversation with Keith, he couldn't help but notice the forty-five-plus trophies and awards displayed around the massive fireplace in the racer's living room. Keith was undoubtedly a winner and was becoming a "legend in his own time." The following are some of Keith's racing accomplishments: the Lakes Region Sled Dog Club awards (first in the World Championship Race 2002 at 2:53:35 and three second place and five third place finishes); the John H. Lyman Best in New Hampshire (fastest heat, best-conditioned team and best leaders); first in the 2005 Open World Championship for the International Federation Sled Dog Race; and five first place finishes in the Eastern North America Race, with three wins in a row from 2003 to 2005.

> *"Now the day had come—my second memorable victory!" The World Championship Race 2011—a strong team and master driver, Keith could not be beaten during the three days of this race in Laconia. His solid run of 2:29:06 in the Open Class was an emotional victory and a sweet first place in the derby.*

## KEITH BRYAR SR.

### *By Cynthia Molburg*

Keith Bryar was born in Laconia, New Hampshire, on October 31, 1925. As a youth, he dreamed of winning the Laconia Championship Sled Dog Race...a dream that was to become a reality.

In 1963, Bryar stormed across the finish line with little more victory margin than a wet husky's nose. But the crowning ceremony had a familiar ring, for Keith had won the 1960 and 1962 World Championship races. That year, with his third win, the tall, trim and handsome Laconia native retired the large, silver Paul Revere winner's bowl over a highly competitive field of American and Canadian dog drivers.

Keith used to skip school on Friday, the first leg of the race. While other boys in other parts of the country dreamed of growing up to become another Hank Greenberg or Joe DiMaggio, Bryar's heart pounded when he thought of matching the feats of Ovide Carrier or Phillip Daigle, Canadians who took Laconia's sled dog honors back in the 1930s, when the contest was in its early stages.

Boyhood ambitions like these often lack both proportion and direction, but they generally are as wholesome as fresh milk, and it is gratifying to discover at least one man who took the trouble to live up to his. This and more Bryar had done. He was the only three-time World Championship winner and had retired the coveted trophy. Additionally, he owned the course speed record for the twenty-mile urban course, better than eighteen miles per hour for the full sixty miles.

Bryar had been racing competitively since 1950, and he devoted a full four months of the year to racing his team. There were a dozen or so contest runs each year in New England—the Laconia event being the last and most

# Introducing Famous Drivers

Keith Bryar Sr. at the World Championship Derby in Laconia, New Hampshire.

important of the series—and there were sled dog races in Canada and Alaska as well. Bryar participated in all of these and often crossed the finish line as the winner.

He operated his own kennel to raise and train his dogs, but neither raising nor racing them earned his means of livelihood. His prize money, such as the $1,000 for first place at Laconia, only contributed to his expenses in following the sport. It was a partnership in Belknap Tire Company in Laconia that provided for his bread and butter.

For all his sled dog victories, Bryar allowed himself very little credit. "I'm a lazy driver," he said. "I give the dogs their full head and let them race. Most of the time, I just ride the sled."

What he failed to say was that to operate this way, you've got to have top dogs, and finding and developing them is where much of the real talent is required. Almost every one of his animals was handpicked from Alaska's ample supply of racing dogs.

Bryar spent a great deal of time conditioning his twelve- to thirteen-dog team, carefully positioning its members along the gang line. If they are correctly placed, each dog could accomplish its job without stress. The "wheels" (the two immediately in front of the sled) dig hard for maximum pull. The "points" (the two immediately behind the lead dog) sprint to support the lead's burst of speed. The "swings" are those pairs of dogs between the point and the wheel dogs that helped to maintain the pace and keep the line taut. The lead is responsible for many things—obeying the driver's commands in order to keep the team on the trail, avoiding obstacles and setting the pace.

Keith credited the lead dog's performance for 60 percent of his successes and 90 percent in the close race, as it was in the 1963 world championship. His inexperienced leader, a two-year-old named Brandy, was evidence of Keith's ability to recognize the qualities of a great racing dog. As it was with Bryar's famous Kimmie, a border collie leader that had been retired. Brandy had earned a front seat in Bryar's dog truck as they traveled from race to race.

Just two years after his Laconia victory, Bryar's racing career was capped successfully in Fairbanks, Alaska, in the three-day North American Championship Race featuring two twenty-mile heats and a final thirty-mile heat. Keith's team emerged victorious after seventy miles of racing

Presentation of trophies. *From left to right*: Paul Jordon, Keith Bryar, Governor Wesley Powell, Musher Queen, Ernie Brunet (winner) and Mayor Ollie Huot, Laconia, New Hampshire.

## Introducing Famous Drivers

in an unusually mild forty-degree temperature for all three days. The New Hampshire man had finished with a lead of 3.36 minutes over the time set by the team driven by the legendary Dr. Roland Lombard of Massachusetts. Bryar's total time was 304.69 minutes, and Lombard was clocked at 307.33 minutes. George Attla from the village of Huslia had been the spectator favorite, but the native Alaskan scratched after his second twenty-mile run, along with five other competitors.

Before heading home, Keith Bryar sold his team to Alaskan dog driver Bill Sullivan, ending an exceptional sled dog racing career. He was out of dog racing and, as it turned out, out of a relationship with his wife, Jean.

In the ensuing years, Keith married Rose and made his home in Arizona. With Rose, Keith returned to his hometown to take up his original calling as a Baptist minister, a mission he had served well in Sandwich, New Hampshire, before he became a headliner in the sled dog world. Just south of Laconia, in Loudon, Bryar built and managed a motorcycle/auto racetrack, which today features National Association Stock Car Auto Racing and Laconia's famous motorcycle race, a weeklong celebration.

Keith Bryar died in 1991 after a losing battle with cancer. Today, his legacy is carried on by his sons, Greg and Keith II. Greg, born during Bryar's first marriage, is the owner-manager of the Balknap Tire Company, and Keith II operates a kennel of sled dogs. He is a top placer on the American and Canadian trails, and in 2002, he, like his dad, claimed victory in the Laconia race over a competitive field of Canadian and American drivers.

### FLORENCE M. CLARK

Back in the days when the Clarks competed in sled dog derbies and town carnivals, the best-known lead dog, Clarkson, which led Florence Clark's team up the statehouse steps during the memorable Berlin-to-Boston trip in the early 1920s, was a most helpful factor in the grind up Mount Washington in 1932.

After eight hours of climbing Mount Washington, Florence Clark completed her third, and this time successful, attempt to drive a team of five Eskimo sled dogs to the top of the mountain. The day was April 3, 1932. She was the first woman to drive a sled dog team to the summit of Mount Washington and back. Clarkson, her female lead dog, led the team of five dogs during the eight-hour climb to the summit. Mrs. Clark also had the distinction of being the only woman to participate in the five-day race from Berlin to Boston in the late 1920s.

# A History of Dog Sledding in New England

Florence Clark and her Eskimo dog team, Woodstock, New Hampshire.

According to the *New Hampshire Sunday News* of January 11, 1948, Mrs. Clark was featured in this article as "The Woman of the Week." The only woman who ever reached the top of Mount Washington with a dog team, Mrs. Clark is a woman among women. The article reads as follows:

> *This trip was known as a hazardous undertaking, and Mrs. Clark attempted it on three different occasions in the winter season. Her last and successful trip was made alone—with only her dog team for company.*
>
> *But Mrs. Clark had a surprise in store for her when she reached the summit after a perilous trip. Coming down from the top of the White Mountain National Forest, Bob Monahan assisted her to the summit and took pictures for her along the way. He protested at the idea of remaining at the top over night; however, informing her that a storm was brewing and that they were to leave immediately. He gave her but fifteen minutes to rest at the little hut on the summit, and then the downward trip began.*
>
> *Mrs. Clark was so tired that she scarcely remembered the details of the trip back, but she did remember that she had promised to light one red flare when she reached the Half-Way House if all was well as she did the previous night. She was to put out two red flares if in distress. Because of the reflection in the snow and ice, those watching below thought they saw two red flares, and feared an accident of some sort had occurred. A group of men started up the trail, but they found no accident—only a very tired but happy young woman who in the glow*

# Introducing Famous Drivers

A team of Ed Clark's Eskimo sled dogs in action.

*of Bob Monahan's cap light, was unable to say anything more than, "I did it!"*

*During World War II, she saw her two young sons, Edward and Murray, go on secret missions for an allied government, and on one notable occasion, she herself, blazed a blizzard to deliver a consignment of Eskimo dogs to a ship in New York, for work overseas.*

*"A credit of honor to any State," was the tribute paid to Mrs. Clark by a representative of an allied government after she had successfully delivered a consignment of about 40 Eskimo dogs to the docks in New York despite the bad weather conditions. Setting out in the stormy weather was nothing new for a small but sturdy Mrs. Clark, but when she assumed the responsibility for delivering the dog to the New York docks in time for shipment overseas, she had just recovered from a small illness.*

*In 1928 Florence and her husband Ed Clark opened a roadside attraction for White Mountain travelers in Lincoln, New Hampshire. "Ed Clark's Eskimo Sled Dog Ranch," featured guided tours of the purebred Eskimo sled dogs and artifacts from the far North. The original "Stand" or Trading Post, offered souvenirs, tonic and maple candy to the motorists on nearby Route 3.*

During their sled dog career, Florence and Edward Clark actively continued racing in the local town carnivals throughout the state.

# A History of Dog Sledding in New England

## Dr. Roland Lombard

An unknown man who was still in high school left the starting line at a race in a small New England town on February 20, 1930, with a team that consisted of two Siberian huskies (left behind by one of the greatest mushers of all time, Leonhard Seppala), two mongrels and a lead dog named Bucky, which was half cocker and half collie. On February 22, after three twenty-mile heats, this same young man had won his first Laconia World Championship handicap race.

Dr. Lombard was competing against some of the country's top drivers and should have been left behind on the trail in the first mile. The snow was fresh and fairly deep; it supported light dogs fairly well. Young Lombard's dogs were very light. The heavier dogs sank, and their tongues began hanging from the labor of dragging themselves out of the snow at each step. At every "Gee!" and "Haw!" from Lombard, his lead dog Bucky smartly swung right or left for better footing. The two Siberians ran as if they were on snowshoes, and whenever the wheel dogs had trouble, the two huskies pulled them right along.

That evening, as Lombard was feeding his dogs, Emile St. Godard, a top Canadian musher, approached him and examined the front paws of one of his Siberians. The pad was distinctive. Besides its snowshoe-like spread, it wasn't bare like most dog pads. It was practically a ball of thick fur, serving as a cushion and providing warmth. The Canadian knew instantly where Lombard had acquired two such dogs, as he had suffered two defeats at the hands of Leonhard Seppala and his Siberian huskies.

The next two days of the race are now history for Dr. Lombard; he won the final heat with a time of fifteen minutes to spare.

The $1,000 he won in that race helped put him through veterinary college and led to a prosperous business, which gave him a chance to pursue his hobby of sled dog racing.

Dr. Lombard's accomplishments since that day in 1930 would fill many pages. He had won the Fairbanks North American Championship six times, the Anchorage Fur Rendezvous Championship seven times and became the holder of many international titles. He and his once famous lead dog Nellie are listed among the sled dog greats, and both have been named to the Knik Mushers Hall of Fame.

Dr. Lombard was a very active participant in the New England Sled Dog Club. He found time to be a past president of the club, of which he had been a member longer than any other driver. He also served for six years as president of the International Sled Dog Racing Association.

## Introducing Famous Drivers

Roland Lombard of Wayland, Massachusetts, racing in the World Championship Derby, 1950s.

## JOHN LYMAN

Russ Armstrong has provided a fine reflection of the Lyman family in his *Sled Dog Generations of Lymans* (April 2006):

> *During World War II, the Laconia sled dog languished and years thereafter until the second generation of dog sledding Lymans. John, together with Keith Bryar Sr., promoted the resurgence of the race in 1956. Sponsored by the Belknap County Sportsman Club, the race immediately attracted an international gathering of professional racers from across the United States and Canada. The race was started downtown, again being the main event of the Laconia Winter Carnival. One can see in the picture here that races were plagued by a paucity of snow even back then.*
>
> *John Lyman trained a team of flying Irish setters, which he loved so much. Although not well suited to competing in the rigors of the race, they were well trained and attracted much attention and admiration from the local citizenry. Largely with the encouragement of John Lyman and Keith Bryar, the Laconia World Championship Sled Dog Race re-established itself as the premier winter*

John Lyman racing his Irish setters on Main Street at the Laconia World Championship Sled Dog Race, circa 1960s.

> *attraction in the Lakes Region. In 1957, former members of the Laconia Sled Dog Club joined to form the Lakes Region Sled Dog Club, which continues today.*

## JIM LYMAN

*President, Lakes Region Sled Dog Club of Laconia, New Hampshire*

Jim Lyman was born in August 1957 and has been around dogs all his life. His grandfather, Charles Lyman, started the World Championship Sled Dog Derby and the Lakes Region Sled Dog Club. Jim's father, John Lyman, bred and raced Irish setters.

At a young age, Jim was not interested in racing the setter breed; rather, he liked the huskies and eventually started his own team with dogs given him by Keith Bryar Sr. and Charlie Posy. In Jim's youth, he raced in the three-dog class for several years and usually placed in the top three. The schedule of races was full, and his family traveled throughout New England, attending a different event each weekend.

Eventually, Jim (nine years old) began building his own training trails and also assisted his father in building the World Championship Trail. Gradually,

## Introducing Famous Drivers

Jim Lyman running Norvik Kennel's second team on the Laconia trail, 2005.

his father got out of the kennel and racing business in the mid-1970s, so Jim's racing participation also ended at that time.

After Jim graduated from Plymouth State College, he decided to become more involved again with the sport. Because of his family background with the World Championship, he officially joined the Lakes Region Sled Dog Club in 1982 and was soon elected club treasurer. He eventually became vice-president, and since 2003, he has been elected president of the club. It is interesting to note that Jim has been the trail boss for the past twenty-five years.

During this time, Jim became friends with Keith Bryar II, who was looking for help in training his dogs. Jim said, "I jumped at the opportunity and have been handling and racing his second-string team ever since. My goals are to help Keith win the World Championship once again and also keep the race going as one of the longest-running races in the lower forty-eight."

For many weeks before each Laconia race, the Lyman Construction Company of Gilford bulldozes and packs the trails, with final checks of the course made just minutes prior to each race.

## Emile Martel "Ole Fox"

### *As told by his daughter, Theresa*

Emile Martel was born on October 22, 1905, in Loretteville, Quebec, Canada. He was raised on a large cattle farm by his parents, Mr. and Mrs. Alfred Martel. From a family of nine brothers and one sister, he was the only son who ever raced in competition. At the age of seventy-four, his dad went out on the trail and even accompanied Emile on his dog racing trips to Laconia and Ottawa. As a young man on the farm, Emile became fond of his dogs. "Seems like I have always had a dog," said Emile.

In the year 1927, a friend gave Emile a dog by the name of Game. Game was part St. Bernard and part Great Dane. Emile and Game became the best of friends; they were always together. One day, Emile had his canoe out on Tile River where the rapids were very high, and Game was swimming along following the canoe, which was a good thing for Emile, for his canoe tipped over and Emile went under. When he came up, his faithful friend Game grabbed him and swam to safety.

Emile went to many races with his brother. He spoke to the mushers and asked questions, but most of the time he was just a silent watcher. He used to watch the "pros" at work, men like Emile St. Godard and Leonhard Seppala. He admired them and the way they worked their teams.

One day, Emile decided to give it a try. He made harnesses, two sleds and was finally ready for competition. Racing with him a few times were Emile St. Godard and Seppala. He was in one race with these two men and came

## Introducing Famous Drivers

in tenth out of twenty-six mushers. Of this race, Emile said, "This is one to remember. My lead dog in the race was Moose; he was the best dog in the team. Good thing I had Moose or I never would have finished tenth. Yes, Moose was my greatest lead dog."

In 1930, Emile won his first derby. It was Emile St. Godard who was the first to congratulate him. Leonhard Seppala said to him, "I knew you could do it. With your patience and the care you give your dogs, it's plain to see that they like you." Emile also took first place in the Laconia Championship Race in 1931 and 1933.

In 1935, Emile raced in Quebec. The race was 120 miles long. He started out with seven dogs. The last day, he had three dogs when he finished. He came in second with a total time of eleven hours, seventeen minutes and twenty-two seconds. His lead was Moose.

In 1957, Emile was the only musher from Quebec ever to participate in La Pas, Manitoba. He came in second. Emile won the International Sled Dog Derby in Quebec seven times.

When Emile came to Laconia to race in 1935, he finished second. It was not until 1957 that he won the World Championship Race. He finished second in 1958 and fourth in 1960. That was the year his dogs were named best-conditioned dog team. He was the first Canadian ever to be awarded this trophy. His team was composed of only four hounds. He started the race with five dogs and finished with five. Little Jess, as he called her, was the lead at the time. Emile was always proud to drive under the *Laconia Evening Citizen* and the Byse Agency banners in the Laconia Derby. Jess started to race at the early age of nine months.

When Emile raced in Ottawa, Jess was only part of the team; later, she moved up to the lead position, where she performed at her best. Jess led six strong crossbreeds, and obedience was one of her better traits.

Jess loved it when Emile went to her before a race. She used to jump on him as if to say, "Master, I'm ready if you are." Emile would often say, "B'gar, she was a good lead dog." His team was never formed of more than seven to nine dogs, and he was good to them all.

Emile raced in about 125 races. One day, he retired, hung up his harness and put away his sled. The Quebec Sled Dog Club gave quite a party in his honor. It was a wonderful party, and among the many guests were Mr. and Mrs. Charles Lyman of Laconia. Together they reminisced about the good old times.

Two years after his retirement, there was a little race for the veteran mushers in Lac Beauport, Quebec. Lucien Therein loaned him three dogs, and sure enough he won the race. He was out of breath when he finished and was sure glad to see the finish line and to be back on the sled once more. No more racing for Emile.

One of the last honors bestowed upon Emile was that of honorary judge of the Laconia World Championship Sled Dog Derby of 1971. He said, "To think that the Lakes Region Sled Dog Club has asked me to be guest of honor at the Laconia Derby, and then the committee of Knik, Alaska, nominated me to the Hall of Fame."

## DEBORAH MOLBURG

*A Legend in Her Own Time*

*Much of this article was created by Team Temakwa.*

Deborah was born in Laconia, New Hampshire, to a family with deep roots in sled dog racing. Deborah Molburg ran her first race in 1956, behind Pavlov, the family pet St. Bernard. From there, she went on to become a top contender in the junior race circuit, sanctioned by the New England Sled Dog Club.

The duo did not win the race that day, but the event is remembered as the day Deborah's love for the sport began. No one could have guessed that it would be the beginning of a lifelong journey into the world of sled dogs and racing ranging from World Championship sprint racing to the challenges of the one-thousand-mile Yukon Quest and the Iditarod Trail Races in Alaska.

Being one of the few female mushers of her time, Deborah had more than her fair share of challenges on and off the trail. Nothing slowed that lady down, and by 1969, Deborah had made herself noticed by claiming two fourth place finishes and one second place finish in the Open Championship Sled Dog Derby in Laconia.

In 1976, Deborah won the Canadian International Championship in Nepean, Ontario. She was the first woman to be awarded an unlimited team medal by the International Sled Dog Racing Association. She was also nominated as Outstanding Athlete of the Year by the *Union Leader* and was featured as Musher of the Year in *Team & Trail* magazine.

The year 1979 brought Deborah back to the starting line where it all began with Pavlov, but this time, things went very differently. Deborah placed first in the World Championship Sled Dog Derby and was the first

## Introducing Famous Drivers

Deborah Molburg racing her dog team in the Laconia World Championship Race.

woman to ever do so. Her success was compounded the following year when Deborah returned to win the derby again. Her time for 1979 was 2:27:27 and in 1980, 1:49:36.

### *Debbie Does It Again*

Variations on the above headline appeared on a regular basis in newspapers and dog sled racing journals throughout New England and eastern Canada during the 1960s, '70s and early '80s as this two-time world sprint champion carved a niche for herself in this competitive arena while succeeding in a sport previously held as a man's domain.

A move to Alaska in 1981 credited the first and longest break in Deborah's dog career, as Juneau's moderate climate was not desirable for training. Deborah retired from sprint racing to put her focus on a canvas business that stays successful to this day. During the early 1990s, Deborah bought property in Tagish, Yukon, and once again returned to her first love of running dogs, with the new vision of mid-distance racing. After being the third woman ever to compete in the Percy DeWolfe, a 210-mile race from Dawson City to Eagle, Deborah was uncertain about mid-distance racing.

Deborah continued to train and run mid-distance races, which eventually led her to the challenging one-thousand-mile Yukon Quest, which she completed in the year 2000 at the age of fifty-five, earning herself the traditional Red Lantern for being the last musher to cross the finish line. Deborah was twenty-first of twenty-nine participants, the others having scratched earlier in the race.

Deborah's latest interest began to take form in 2006, when she and her husband, Sandy, flew into various checkpoints of the Iditarod Trail. It was not long before Deborah had set her sights on running another thousand-mile race. She made her first attempt in 2007 with a leased team from Agata Franczak and completed three hundred miles before she decided to withdraw from the race after taking a wrong trail during a blizzard. This, however, did not deter Deborah; it only made her want to finish more. So for the 2008 season, she purchased fourteen of her team dogs and borrowed dogs from William Kleedhen in hopes of training a successful Iditarod team. Deborah was both nervous and excited about the race, but as always, she carried with her the confidence of an experienced dog driver. When the announcer said, "Go!" she would do what she knew best and drive her dogs toward Nome, Alaska. Deborah finished the 2008 race in fifteen days, five hours, thirty-six minutes and twelve seconds.

Anyone acquainted with this fine lady musher and the focus she gives any objective will offer this advice: don't be against her!

## RICHARD (DICK) MOLBURG

### *By Cynthia Molburg*

Richard Molburg was born in Whitefield, New Hampshire, on May 13, 1924. Throughout his youth and as an adult, he was fascinated by the outdoor challenges offered by the lakes and woods of his native home. As an independent man, he preferred tending to his trap lines to working in an office or production plant, and as a result of his success in the field, he was often sought out by the New Hampshire Fish & Game Department.

In his teens, he lived with his family in The Weirs and spent much of his time fishing from a boat in the summer and from a bob house on the frozen surface of Lake Winnipesaukee in the winter. He was a Laconia High School student, and in February 1943, he joined the U.S. Army. While in the service, he married Cynthia Dekker, his high school sweetheart. As a young girl, Cynthia devoured Jack London stories and poems by Robert Service; thus, it was no wonder that Dick, an enthusiastic spectator at the early Laconia races, was somehow led into the real world of sled dogs.

During the war years, when many of the competitors in the Laconia derby were serving in the armed forces, the race was put on hold. When it returned to the city in 1956, a "mutt" derby was added to the main event—a race for children and their family pets. Among the competitors in that race

# Introducing Famous Drivers

Richard and Cynthia Molburg as they celebrate their daughter's sled dog victory.

were Dick's eleven-year-old daughter Deborah and her St. Bernard, Pavlov. From that small beginning, dad, mom and all six of their children were to become heavily involved in the sport.

Not long after that first race experience, the Molburgs moved a few miles north to an old homestead in Moultonboro, where there was plenty of room for their six youngsters and an ideal area to raise and train sled dogs. Just a short mile away, the Bryars of New England sled dog racing fame had established a well-known kennel of racing dogs. It was not long before the two families got together, and Dick became a regular dog handler, working with Keith Bryar on training trips that took them into the White Mountains.

While working with Keith, Dick observed and learned how a champion driver trains his dogs, and on the trip back home, he asked Keith hundreds of questions, which included everything from equipment, how to determine where to place a dog on the gang line, how he decided the miles to be run on a given day, etc. Dick was getting a priceless education.

Dick and Cindy guided their offspring to successful finishes on the New England junior circuit in the 1960s, when the club included one hundred kids with their one- and three-dog teams. The competition was keen, and with half a dozen Molburg junior mushers on the trails, they took home more than their share of trophies. During that period, their Temakwa

## A History of Dog Sledding in New England

Kennel expanded to include several bloodlines, including the original Bryar Siberians infused with bloodlines from dogs dating back to Roland Lombard's Igloo Pac racing kennel, which had established an unbroken record of wins by an "outsider" in the classic Alaskan races; John Lyman's team of Irish setters, which was a consistent top finisher in Laconia races; and Canadian hounds, which dominated the early Laconia and Quebec championship derbies for several years. It became known as the "Big-Yapper" line, two of the outstanding dogs in the breeding program.

By the 1970s, Dick's breeding program was paying off, and his dogs were recognized throughout North America. They were not only fast, but they were also tough and could handle the long sprint racing trails under almost any weather and trail conditions. The team's crowning achievements occurred in the '70s. In the 1976 three-day Canadian Championship in Nepean, Quebec, Dick's daughter Deborah drove a fourteen-dog team on the 22.5-mile trail to claim victory over three former Laconia champions, Dick Moulton, Harris Dunlap and Eddy Sylvain. In 1979, the Molburg team won the World Championship Sled Dog Derby in Laconia, again piloted by Deborah, the first woman to win the race in its fiftieth-anniversary year. In 1980, the Molburg team, with Deborah at the helm, successfully defended its title.

Dick's talents were to expand beyond training and breeding sled dogs in the '70s. Cindy, a charter member of the International Sled Dog Racing Association, had to drag Dick into the organization despite his cynicism. His peers convinced him that if the sport was to gain international recognition and sponsors, it needed leaders who could design and enforce uniform race rules and procedures. Dick was appointed sanctioning chairman when the program began in 1970 and served in that capacity for ten years. Sometimes controversial, Dick set high standards for ISDRA-sanctioned events and held race organizations responsible for the quality of them. He also was elected to the board of directors for multiple terms as both a regional and at-large representative. He held the office of treasurer and was the organization's first executive officer. During those years of service, he was very influential, and in 1986, he and Cindy, who had served ISDRA in several capacities, were named two of the association's then eleven honorary members.

Little did Dick know when he encouraged Cindy to take over *Team & Trail*, a monthly sled dog publication, in 1967 that he was committing himself to an office job as its manager and editorial writer for the next forty-seven years. Under the guidance of the Molburgs, *Team & Trail*'s extensive race coverage, news and advertisements attracted subscribers from throughout the world. As a result, it encouraged dog drivers to travel great distances to race their teams in events spanning North America, many drivers coming from as far away as Europe.

With his wife at his side, Dick Molburg died of heart failure at his home on January 27, 2005. When he reached the finish line, he left behind a legacy of many colorful stories and contributions to the sport, six self-sufficient offspring in many fields of endeavor and a countless number of friends who had traveled with him on and off the sled dog trails.

## ED MOODY

Ed Moody was considered the dean of sled dog racing. He had competed in races all over the country, trained and drove dogs for Admiral Byrd's 1933 expedition, trained army and air force sled dogs in Colorado and Greenland and had been making sleds for over forty-five years. His sled making was squeezed into his off hours from his regular job as a service representative for Nalew's, Inc., a construction engineering company in Laconia, New Hampshire. There was never time to fill all the incoming orders, and a Moody sled was hard to come by—a status symbol in the sled dog sport.

Dr. Jim Corbin, Purina pet care center director, describes Moody as a "likable, highly energetic dog lover, who was probably the best dog sled maker in America. He even sold sleds to Eskimos."

A reporter for the Ralston Purina Co. asked the following questions in an interview during the 1960s:

> *Q. You've been involved in sled dog racing since you were a boy. What's your opinion of the state of the sport today?*
> *Moody. It's better and getting better every year. The petty jealousies of years ago are gone. People used to pull stunts to make you lose a race, like driving their car in front of your dogs. Even though there are money prizes today, the relations between drivers are excellent. Also there were enough races so that the same teams can't make them all.*
>
> *Brutality to the dogs was once a problem with some drivers, but the clubs have stiffened the rules. If a whip is used, it can't be more than three feet long and not used to abuse the dogs. A driver must bring back all the dogs he started with and can't substitute dogs on succeeding days of a race.*
> *Q. Why have you worked with dogs for so many years, what has it meant for you?*
> *Moody. The satisfaction I get out of dogs is training them so I can handle them. I've been in situations where my life depended on a dog's obedience.*

# A History of Dog Sledding in New England

*Q. Did such "situations" occur on the Byrd expedition?*
Moody. Yes, more than once.
*Q. What made you join the expedition?*
Moody. I was a kid off the farm—I wanted to see what was on the other side of the mountain: I still do. It was a 10,000-mile trip, all for free, and so were my services. I just thought about what I would see, not what I was leaving

In 1933 there weren't many people anywhere with experience driving dogs. I'd had experience and that was the main reason I was taken. When I got a team trained and going good, I'd turn them over to other drivers.
*Q. What was the biggest problem you had to overcome on the trip?*
Moody. The weather—blizzards, crevasses, ice breaks. The worst was unloading the ship at the Bay of Whales. We had just so much time until the bay froze. Nine dog teams were hauling 1,000 pounds a load, much more than their own weight—we just worked until we couldn't anymore.

We found that 60 below was the coldest we could work the dogs. Below that their lips and feet pads froze. The coldest I remember was 72 degrees below. A plane went down and I was asked to bring them gas and oil by dog team.

It wasn't far from our main base, "Little America," but I had to travel all the next two days to get there. It was so cold I couldn't sleep. I dug holes and buried the dogs in the snow, but forgot to tie my lead dog. He laid against me that night and somehow didn't get frost bit.
*Q. How important were the dogs to the success of the expedition?*
Moody. Admiral Byrd called them the backbone of the expedition. At that time we couldn't have gotten along without them. Mechanical equipment was better when it was working, but the tractors broke down and the dogs kept going.

They also had a moral value for the men. Dogs have personalities and even the men who didn't drive knew and liked various dogs. Many brought their favorites home with them.
*Q. When and why did you start making sleds?*
Moody. I made my first sled in 1923. At that time I had no power tools at all. My reason was simple, I needed a good dog sled and no one made dog sleds. People kept asking for them so kept making them.
*Q. How long did it take to make a sled?*
Moody. Once I've made all the parts, I could put one together in a little over a day. I'm able to make 12–14 sleds a year and since Dr. Lombard has a standing order for eight, the waiting list is long.

I'm milling parts right now and probably won't assemble any sleds 'til the fall.
*Q. What's used in a sled?*

*Moody. I use white ash or hickory. It's hard to get the high quality wood I need. The curved parts must be steamed. Rawhide lashing is used instead of screws and bolts to give the sled flexibility.*

## DICK MOULTON

A native of Meredith, Dick doesn't say much, but when he does, it's usually something about sled dog racing. Dick began his interest in dog racing at the early age of nine. With many years of training, racing and breeding his dogs, he became an experienced veteran sled dog driver and trainer from Center Harbor, New Hampshire. He has probably logged as many miles behind a sled as any man alive today, and if there's anything he doesn't know about driving dogs, it probably isn't worth knowing.

Despite his long backlog of experience, there isn't a touch of arrogance in his attitude, which explains why a man who passed about everyone on the trail during the three-day race was selected as the outstanding sportsman by all his fellow drivers.

When Dick received the Leonhard Seppala Memorial Trophy back in 1968, he was typically reticent, saying, "I don't really think that I deserve this. There were so many drivers who helped by giving me a clear field to pass that I couldn't have won without fine sportsmanship."

This respect Dick showed for other drivers was returned in their respect for him as a master driver. He was labeled Man of the Year by the Canadian drivers, and he more than lived up to the billing, posting the best time each day of the '68 race by setting a course record with his Friday time of one hour, eight minutes and fifty-five seconds for the twelve-mile course. His overall time for the three-day, sixty-mile derby was three hours, thirty-five minutes and eight seconds, another record.

Dick had raced in almost all of the top money races around the country but never won a major race until 1968—the Laconia World Championship Derby. Dick's time for the 1968 championship race was 3:35:08; for the 1971 race, 4:17:45; for 1973, 3:38:09; for 1975, 4:01:36; and for 1976, 2:17:28.

He drove a large team of seventeen dogs. His team, for the most part, was young and figured to be a top threat for many years to come.

In his early years, he became so proficient at handling dogs that he was offered a chance to make the Antarctic Expedition with Admiral Byrd. Upon accepting, he was later awarded a Congressional Medal of Honor for his work at the South Pole.

# A History of Dog Sledding in New England

Dick Moulton (left) receiving the World Championship Sled Dog Derby trophy from Governor Meldrim Thompson Jr. and Chief Judge Reg Boudin.

During World War II, Dick served with the Army Sled Dog Division.

In addition to the Governor's Trophy and the Seppala Memorial, he also won the Charles H. Lyman Trophy as the best New Hampshire driver and literally hundreds of other noteworthy trophies and prizes from around the continent. One of the finest tributes he received came from fellow driver J. Malcolm McDougall of St. Agathe, Quebec, the second place finisher. McDougall observed at the awards ceremony of the '68 race that "outside myself, there's no one I'd rather see win than Dick Moulton." From the response that remark got from the other drivers, the sentiment appeared to be unanimous.

Dick retired from racing in the early 1980s and was instrumental in the formation and running of the Siberian Evaluation Performance Project—an annual event held between 1982 and 1990. Dick, along with Dr. Lombard and Charlie Belford, evaluated the running qualities of many Siberians, and most, if not all, serious Siberian racing enthusiasts of the 1980s attended these events at one time or another to spend hours listening to and picking the brains of Dick, Doc and Charlie. The SEPP evaluation did much to help identify the truly good working Siberians of a decade ago. Dick died in 2000; however, he will always be remembered as a musher who did it all.

# Introducing Famous Drivers

## Elizabeth Ricker

Married to the son of the family that owned Poland Spring Hotel in Maine, Elizabeth was introduced to sled dogs by watching Arthur Walden and his Chinook team. She bought a team of dogs from Walden but traded her Chinook team for Siberian huskies when she met Seppala. Eventually, she married a second time, to Kaare Nansen, the son of a famous Arctic explorer, and lived out her life in Ottawa, Canada. She never lost her love or enthusiasm for sled dogs and the sport of sled dog racing. She wrote two well-known books, *Toga's Fireside Reflections* and *Seppala, Alaskan Dog Driver*, which remain classics in Siberian husky research and study. She is credited with putting forth the idea of an international governing body for sled dog racing that grew into the formation of the ISDRA.

## Eva "Short" Seeley

Eva "Short" Seeley needs no introduction in the sport of sled dog racing, for her famous Chinook Kennels are well known all over the world and were one of the outstanding tourist attractions in the state of New Hampshire.

Eva Seeley came to New Hampshire on her honeymoon and, along with her husband, Milton Seeley, purchased the Chinook Kennels during the early 1920s. During the Antarctica Expedition and seven other expeditions on United States assignments, the Chinook Kennels played an important role. She was the only woman who had been appointed chief consultant for the United States Antarctica Deepfreeze Expedition. Not only were the dogs trained for their wonderful works at the South Pole but so were the many drivers who served under Admiral Byrd.

Mrs. Seeley was a highly distinguished AKC judge of Siberian huskies, Samoyed and Alaskan malamutes. She founded the Siberian Husky Club and the Alaskan Malamute Club. She was honored as president of the Siberian Husky Club of America. "Short" Seeley was a charter member of the New England Sled Dog Club in 1924 and an honorary member of the International Sled Dog Club Racing Association (ISDRA). She was the only woman to participate in the 1930s Olympic Sled Dog Demonstration at Lake Placid, New York, along with such noted drivers as Leonhard Seppala, Emile St. Godard, Colonel Norman Vaughan and Roger Haines.

Mrs. Seeley's accomplishments in the sled dog sport are too numerous to mention in this short resumé but have endeared her to the hearts of many of the dog drivers racing today. Her interest and promotion of the

# A History of Dog Sledding in New England

Mrs. Eva "Short" Seeley's dog team in the White Mountains National Forest foothill in Wonalancet, framed by the Sandwich Range in the background, circa 1938.

Junior Sled Dog Racing program helped to produce some of the finest sled dog drivers in the East.

## Leonhard Seppala

*Jonathan N. Hayes from the Poland Spring Kennel has provided the following profile of Leonhard Seppala.*

Leonhard Seppala was born in Skibotn, Norway, in the summer of 1877. It was in 1899 that a friend of Leonhard's told him about the riches of gold in Alaska. The lure of wealth and adventure was just too much for the twenty-two-year-old man, and he traveled to Alaska for a new beginning.

Shortly after his arrival in Alaska, Seppala was given the opportunity to take a dog team out prospecting for gold. The two one-hundred-pound mongrels were the best way to travel in this frozen tundra. This new experience was the beginning of a new life—an adventure as a musher.

# Introducing Famous Drivers

In 1908, Nome, Alaska, organized its Nome Kennel Club, and the thirty-one-year-old Seppala was ready for his first race.

Leonhard Seppala tells the story that he won this first race due to the intervention of a buzzard. The story goes that the buzzard kept landing in the trail just ahead of his team. The team would pour on the steam to catch the lure, only to be teased by the bird flying away at the last moment. The buzzard would then land again in the trail just ahead. Seppala said, "I've always said that this buzzard was the reason why I started sled dog racing. The fact that I won that race started my career as a sled dog racer."

The next year, the Nome Kennel Club ran its second annual five-hundred-mile All-Alaska Sweepstakes Race. Seppala was not yet ready to participate in this race. Everyone looking on was quite amused when a Russian fur trader, William Goosak, pulled into the starting shoot with some half-sized, bushy tailed rat dogs, which he had imported from Siberia. The odds were set at one hundred to one against these Siberian runts. However, everyone in the Nome Kennel Club was shocked, and the Nome Bank almost bankrupted, when the

Sitting in the sled is Leonhard Seppala, deceased hero of the 1925 Nome serum run and honorary judge at the Laconia Championship Derby, 1962. Keith Bryar Sr. of Laconia, New Hampshire, is seen standing at the rear of the sled.

Siberian dogs came in third place. Onlookers noted that these little dogs seemed as energetic as when they had left the starting shoot. Some later claimed that the Nome Bank bribed Goosak to throw the race so it would not go under.

Seppala received his first team of Siberian husky imports from his employer to be trained in 1913, a few years after the first import by Goosak and the subsequent import of Siberians by Charles Ramsey. Seppala raced with these young Siberian dogs the next year in the All Alaska Sweepstakes Race but had to scratch due to a blinding blizzard. This did not discourage him, however, for he won the Sweepstakes the following three consecutive years. These three wins made him and his Siberian huskies famous. But Seppala was not through yet.

He probably would have continued to dominate the Sweepstakes race if it had not been put to an abrupt end with many sled dogs being deported to Europe. The world had been drawn into World War I. By the time the war ended, air transportation was becoming more of a reality, even in these northern climates, and it would appear that the age of the sled dog was drawing to a close.

It was Jonathan Hayes who said:

> *I have always felt that great men need great challenges in for to shine... If the story of Seppala ended here, we would probably not thinking of him now, nor trying to preserve the breed he worked so hard to establish. Seppala's greatest test was to come in the winter of 1925, when the advent of the airplane was already putting the final nails in the casket of the dog sled transportation.*

A diphtheria epidemic had broken out in Nome, Alaska. "The Strangler," as the disease was commonly called, had come for the children of Nome. The antitoxins Dr. Welch had ordered had not arrived in the last shipment.

Nome was, as it is today, completely closed to the outside world. There were no passable winter roads. The port was iced in for miles. The only way in, then and now, after the snow flies, was by plane. When the temperature dropped below zero degrees, the planes of the 1920s were unreliable and dangerous at best.

There were some brave pilots in Anchorage who wanted to fly in the serum to Nome, but no one had ever been successful traveling such a distance under such conditions. The most reliable way to transport the serum was via sled dogs.

The citizens of Nome suggested that Leonhard Seppala carry the serum. After a town meeting, a phone call was sent to Seppala's home, and the dogs

## Introducing Famous Drivers

began to howl. They asked him to travel toward Nenana, and the serum would be transported to Nenana via train. They wanted the 640 miles between the two towns to be traversed by dog team. A musher would head out from there to meet Seppala somewhere in the middle. Hayes continued:

> *While Seppala was on the trail, the Governor of Alaska picked up the plan, but could not trust the fate of those in Nome to a single musher. So as politicians are apt to do, the Governor complicated the plan to include some twenty teams and mushers in performing a relay. The problem was, how would the traveling Seppala be told he was not to transport it alone?*

Seppala traveled a total of 340 miles to save the children of Nome. Seppala crossed the treacherous sea ice of Norton Sound twice to save time, once heading out to receive the serum and then again on the way back.

As he was instructed, Seppala transferred the serum to the next musher, Gunnar Kaason. Within a year, Seppala and his lead dog, Togo, began to be recognized for their accomplishments. In October 1926, Seppala and his team were brought to the United States for a tour and to be honored in Madison Square Garden with a medal, which would be presented by the famous explorer Roald Amundsen.

Arthur Walden of Wonalancet, New Hampshire, who was an accomplished breeder and racer of the Chinook dog breed, extended an open invitation to Leonhard Seppala to come to his farm and dog kennel to train and possibly participate in races in the New England area.

Leonhard Seppala won the Laconia Championship Sled Dog Derby in 1929.

## EMILE ST. GODARD

Emile St. Godard (1905–1948) was one of the most accomplished sled dog mushers during the 1920s and '30s. He hailed from Winnipeg, Manitoba, Canada.

St. Godard's first major win was at La Pas in 1925, one of the world's premier dog sled races at the time. He would continue to win this race the next five times, until 1929. In 1930, Emile lost the race to Earl Brydges by a margin of twenty and a half minutes.

During his career, he received a citation from the Canadian Federation of Humane Societies for his concern and kindness for his dog team. His lead dog, Toby, was a husky-greyhound crossbreed.

In 1956, he was inducted into Canada's Sports Hall of Fame, and in 2007, he was inducted into the Manitoba Sports Hall of Fame. He remains the only dog sled racer to be recognized by either the national or provincial awards.

## ARTHUR WALDEN

*Breeder, Musher and Promoter of Sled Dog Racing*

Arthur Walden was born in Indianapolis, Indiana, on May 10, 1871. He was educated at Chattuck Military School in Faribault, Minnesota. In March 1896, at the age of twenty-four, he went to Alaska. While in the Yukon, he worked with an Eskimo dog named Chinook, which made a deep impression on him. Later, he returned to New Hampshire and settled in the quaint little hamlet of Wonalancet (Tamworth) with the intention of re-creating the sled dog experience.

On his thirteen-hundred-acre Wonalancet farm, he and his wife, Kate Sleeper, settled, and Arthur Walden began breeding and training sled dogs. His intention was to build friendly, gentle dogs that would have power, endurance and speed. It was here that Walden's lead dog Rikki produced the trait that he wanted. He renamed it Chinook, honoring the Eskimo dogs in the Yukon. It was from this meager beginning that he further promoted the sport of sled dog racing, with Chinook as his lead dog.

According to J. Jeffrey Bragg, authority on the life of Arthur Walden, who wrote an article for the International Seppala Association entitled "Arthur T. Walden, Dog Driver from the Yukon to Antarctica" in 2005:

> *Walden introduced his new line of "husky half-breeds" to the world in 1920 at the Gorham, New Hampshire, Winter Carnival and straightway began to promote his dogs for diverse purposes: racing, heavy freighting and recreation. In the early 1920s, he successfully ascended Mount Washington. This and other stunts won considerable local renown for Walden and Chinook. In 1922, he persuaded a local paper company to sponsor the first Eastern International Dog Derby of 123 miles. He is thus credited with bringing the sport of dog sled racing to New England. In 1924, he spearheaded the founding of the New England Sled Dog Club, which is still in operation today.*

Walden began writing his experiences into what would eventually become three published works. Fresh on the heels of writing his first

## Introducing Famous Drivers

Sled Dog Derby Time, 1925, in Laconia, New Hampshire. *From left to right*: Leonhard Seppala, Dr. Sproull, Arthur Walden and Walter Channing.

book, he went to Boston to meet with Admiral Richard Byrd, and at the age of fifty-eight, Walden was employed by Admiral Byrd and was awarded the position as lead trainer and driver of the dog team for the expedition. Malamutes and husky-type dogs were brought down from Alaska and Canada to augment the expedition teams; young men arrived at the Wonalancet farm to train as dog drivers. The vicinity hummed with the activity of the expedition preparations, and the kennels grew up and expanded so that the tiny hamlets of Wonalancet, Tamworth and Sandwich became known for decades as the "Sled Dog Capital of the World." The Byrd Expedition of 1928 assured Arthur Walden a lasting place in United States history, but it is the title "Father of New England Dog Sledding" that he would cherish most.

J. Jeffrey Bragg continued his chronicle of Walden's expedition with Admiral Richard Byrd:

> *In September 1928, Walden was to be in charge of hauling supplies to support the base camp "Little America."*

# A History of Dog Sledding in New England

> *On January 17, Walden's single team of 13 dogs moved 3,500 lbs of supplies from the ship to the base camp, a distance of 16 miles. Walden's team was the backbone of their transport.*
>
> *Upon returning to his farm in Wonalancet, in 1929, he sold his share of the Chinook Kennels to Milton and Eva B. Seeley.*

On March 26, 1947, a fire broke out in the basement of his Wonalancet farm. He tried desperately to put out the fire, but without success. He was found dead in the kitchen, possibly overcome by smoke. He was certainly a hero, a breeder of prize stock, as seen in Chinook, and an adventurer in the sled dog sport.

The highway marker on the road by his home in Wonalancet reads, "The Chinook Trail"—a continuing reminder of the breed of dog known as the Chinook, a lasting legacy left to us by Arthur Walden and the first Chinook. Their story is one of adventure.

A complete account of Arthur Walden's achievements in the sport and his involvement in the New England Club may be found in chapter one, and more information on Chinook may be found in chapter four.

## Racing Sled Dog Champions

*Cynthia Molburg, editor and publisher of* Team & Trail, *wrote this special article of reminiscent reflections on Dick Moulton, Harris Dunlap and Deborah Molburg for the 1977 World Championship Sled Dog Derby in Laconia, New Hampshire.*

What does a former Admiral Byrd expeditionist have in common with a former art teacher and a lady entrepreneur? The ability to race sled dogs and a strong determination to win in every contest they enter—among them, the World Championship Sled Dog Derby in Laconia, New Hampshire.

Richard Moulton of Center Harbor is the expeditionist; Harris Dunlap of Bakers Mills, New York, is the artist; and Deborah Molburg, also of Center Harbor, is the lady entrepreneur. In 1976, it was these three dog drivers who led the pack on the championship trail covering a total fifty-four miles.

Richard Moulton began his racing career as a youth working his team in the town of Meredith in the 1930s and at the Chinook Kennels in Wonalancet. At that kennel, they were training dogs for Admiral Byrd's third Antarctic Expedition (1939–41), and Moulton became acquainted with the great explorer. He joined Byrd as a team driver in the adventure over the frozen

## Introducing Famous Drivers

wasteland of the South Pole. It might be said of Moulton that he has had one of the more colorful associations with sled dogs, as he followed up the expedition with a hitch in the United States Army during World War II, training dogs for rescue work in the European field.

In 1976, Moulton set an unprecedented record by winning the Laconia race for the fifth time after having captured the race in 1968, 1971, 1973 and 1975. The closest challenge to his record was made by Dr. Charles Belford, of Deerfield, Massachusetts, who was the honorary judge of the 1977 World Championship Race. Moulton was one of the best trainers in the sled dog world, and his years of experience in racing dogs had proven to be tough. His sense of pace and timing and his ability to recognize top running dogs were all on his side in a sport that produced great variations in running conditions.

Moulton's racing activities had taken him into Alaska in addition to winning the Laconia World Championship title. In 1975, he won the International Bronze Medal award of the International Sled Dog Racing Association (ISDRA), making him one of the top three mushers in the world. Such recognition is earned by racing in ISDRA-sanctioned events throughout the world against international competition.

Harris Dunlap, 1982 winner of the Open North American Race. This team photo was taken during the second heat. This is Harris after seventy miles.

Deborah Molburg has been described as the "youngest old-timer" in the sport, having run her first race in Laconia in 1956 with a lone St. Bernard in a mutt derby. From that day on, the young female musher had developed as a dog racer, necessitating that she become a lady entrepreneur in several fields, including seasonal employment and real estate activities during the summer months and trapping and making dog harnesses in the fall. Over the years, she worked her way up through the junior musher ranks into the senior racing circuit, which had taken her into Canada and the midwestern and western states in the USA.

In 1976, Deborah presented the closest challenge offered by a female driver to the reigning champion by winning one heat of the race on the eighteen-mile trail and finishing just a little more than three minutes off the pace for the total fifty-four-mile run. Jean Bryar of Center Harbor was the only other woman to have won a runner-up place in the World Championship, but the interval separating her from the first place teams was nineteen minutes.

As a result of her and her team's top placing in several races, including the winning of the Canadian National Heritage Cup Championship in Nepean, Ontario, Molburg was named Musher of the Year in 1976 by *Team & Trail*. In addition, she was awarded the 1976 International Silver Medal by ISDRA, making her the first female dog driver to be acclaimed as one of the top three mushers in the world

Of the three champions, Harris Dunlap had been racing the least number of years, but his determination to reach the top had overcome that handicap. With more than a dozen years of experience, Dunlap had managed to chalk up several wins and near wins throughout the North American continent, including in Alaska and three second place finishes in Laconia in 1971, 1972 and 1975 and two thirds in 1970 and 1976.

The former New York art teacher gave up his teaching career to devote his time to racing sled dogs. As a result, he became one of the most knowledgeable mushers in the field of nutritional needs of racing sled dogs, working with Dr. David Kronfled, DVM, of the University of Pennsylvania. In addition to his practical and scientific endeavors in the sport of sled dog racing, he was editor of the ISDRA publication *INFO*, which featured articles about the care and training of sled dogs.

After five years of domination by George Attla of Alaska and Dr. Roland Lombard of Massachusetts since 1972, Dunlap emerged to the top of the ranks in international competition, claiming the 1976 ISDRA gold medal. He was the silver medal holder in 1975.

Moulton, Molburg and Dunlap are three of the many sled dog racing champions in the world, and every year new challenges were offered to them by their peers—especially on the Laconia World Championship Sled Dog Derby Trail. The winner of the 1977 World Championship Sled Dog Derby was Harris Dunlap.

Introducing Famous Drivers

## Lady Mushers of the Past

"Women in a man's world" was a cliché characteristic of the new and liberated life of the late twentieth century. Generally, however, women in sports are members of all-female teams playing under a set of rules set up for women.

Lately, we read of a woman who thought she wanted to be a baseball umpire. She tried it but decided it was not for her. However, one sport has existed for many years in which women compete on equal footing with men and under the same rules—namely, sled dog racing. Here is a sport where no concession is made to the female sex, except in Alaska, where it all began. There, the women have their own races. It should be mentioned that the women's races are not for the fainthearted. They are serious and difficult races. Names such as Kit McInnis, Natalie Norris, Rosie Losonsky, Joyce Wells from Alaska and Jean Bryar, Florence Clark, Eva "Short" Seeley, Anne Wing, Louise Lombard, Lorna Demidoff, Millie Turner and Deborah Molburg from the lower forty-eight states have been associated with racing competitions as winners or as good finishers.

In April 3, 1932, Florence Clark was the first woman to drive her team of five Eskimo sled dogs to the top of Mount Washington and back.

In 1949, Louise Lombard was the only woman entered in the ninety-mile Ottawa Dog Sled Derby. She raced in competition with her husband. At the time, she was driving a team of six malamutes led by a Siberian husky named Wolf, which had made a name for himself as one of the army dogs sent over to Europe to be used in the Battle of the Bulge removing the wounded from the battlefield.

Mrs. E.P. Ricker (Mrs. Nansen) drove dogs in 1928. She placed second in the Fourth Annual Sled Dog Derby in Lake Placid in 1931. Her daughter, Bunty Dunlop, also became a good sled dog driver.

Lorna Demidoff of Monadnock Kennels laid claim to being the only female driver to win a New England Sled Dog Race in a period of thirty-one years.

"Short" Seeley of Chinook Kennels, in addition to racing a fine team, participated in the Olympics Exhibition Race in the 1930s at Lake Placid, New York, being the only woman to have that distinction.

At Anchorage, the Women's Champion Rendezvous Race was started in 1953. Joyce Wells drove a team of Targhee hounds to victory in that first race. The next year, Natalie Norris won the race, driving a team of registered Siberian huskies.

Millie Turner of Cold River Kennels drove a Class A team in the New England Sled Dog Club all through the 1930s and early '40s to place well in all the races, including some of the "tough ones" in Canada.

Jean Bryar won the North American Women's Championship at Fairbanks to become the first woman from the lower forty-eight states to achieve this goal. She also competed in many of the grueling Canadian races, as well as Laconia's World Championship Race.

# IV
# CHINOOK

Chinook dogs, originated by Arthur T. Walden of Alaskan, Antarctic and New Hampshire fame, established a breed of sled dogs with tremendous power and endurance combined with a speed of five to ten miles per hour, depending on the size of the load carried. This breed of dog was to be between the huge Alaskan freighter and the much smaller Siberian, which were used on the tundra. The Chinook breed was the result of many years of careful breeding. How well Mr. Walden succeeded is evidenced by the fact that on the first Byrd Antarctic Expedition, the original Chinook team established record after record for loads carried and distances covered. This breed was and still is considered by many to be the ideal type of sled dog for all purposes.

Chinook himself, known the world over as Arthur Walden's famous lead dog, which wandered off and died in the Antarctic at the ripe old age of twelve, was the direct ancestor of all the dogs of the Wonalancet-Hubbard Kennels in New Hampshire.

The Chinook breed was originally established by crossing a Greenland husky with a dog strong in St. Bernard blood. The strain was further carried out by crossing with the working-class type of Shepherd dog. This crossing lightened the weight of the bone inherited from the St. Bernard. As is necessary in establishing a breed of dogs, today there are defined standards of color, height, weight, etc. The purebred Chinook dog is large, averaging from 90 to 110 pounds, with two color phases, the standard a light fawn and the other—very rare—a dark fawn.

# A History of Dog Sledding in New England

Chinook Kennels. Purchased and moved to this site in 1930 by Milton and Eva B. "Short" Seeley, these kennels produced sled dogs for exploration, racing and showing. For almost fifty years, Chinook Kennels exerted a profound influence on the Alaskan malamute and Siberian husky breeds, and many champions were born here. With Milton directing, dog teams were sent on the Byrd Antarctic Expeditions and to the army's Search and Rescue units. After his death in 1943, Eva continued alone. An author, sled dog racer and dynamic contributor to the sport of dog sledding, "Short" was named to the Mushers' Hall of Fame in Alaska. Mrs. Seeley died in 1985 at the age of ninety-four.

## BREEDING

In 1931, after Arthur Walden's return from the Antarctic, Mrs. Julia P. Lombard of Wonalancet, New Hampshire, began breeding Chinook dogs in accordance with the standards established by Mr. Walden. During the time Mr. Walden was standardizing the Chinook breed, Mrs. Lombard raised all his puppies.

While breeding and training these Chinook dogs, Mrs. Lombard realized that they had inherited the affectionate disposition and gentleness of the St. Bernard and found that they readily adapted themselves to any climate and were especially fond of children. The power of Chinook dogs was such that, trained to a sled or cart, one dog can supply many hours of enjoyment for one or two youngsters. It was further found that as a winter sport for all the family, a team of two or three dogs was sufficient to carry food and camping equipment for picnic parties over mountain trails in midwinter.

# Chinook

## "Short" Seeley and the Chinook Dog

So as not to be confused, there were two Chinook Kennels. The first kennel was established by Arthur Walden, with the aide of Mrs. Lombard, and the second was operated under the same name and run by Milton and Eva Seeley. The latter is now famous for both the Alaskan malamute and the Siberian husky breed. The Seeleys' Chinook Kennels was considered the second life of the first Chinook Kennels, founded by Walden about the time everyone wanted dogs like the one he was driving in the races and at winter carnivals. The first Chinook Kennels ceased being owned by Walden and came under full ownership of the Seeleys sometime in the 1930s. The Seeleys moved the kennels from behind the Wonalancet farm up the road to property they had purchased from Walden when they bought out his Wonalancet Electric Company.

After Milton and Eva Seeley took over and relocated the Chinook Kennels, Julia Lombard, an erstwhile partner of Arthur Walden in the Electric Company, formed the Wonalancet Kennels, which raised only Chinook dogs. Julia asked Arthur Walden to direct the kennels for her. In 1940, these kennels, with twenty dogs, were sold to Perry Greene from Maine, who had seen them displayed at sportsmen's shows. He moved the kennels first to

A Chinook team with Milton and Eva Seeley on the sled.

Warren, Maine, and then established Perry Greene's Chinook Kennels on Route 1 in Waldoboro, Maine.

Perry Greene continued Walden's unique method of selecting new owners. Before purchasing a Chinook, Perry required that a prospective owner stay at Perry Greene Kennels for at least twenty-four hours. If the dog did not like the person, he would go home empty-handed. If the person passed this scrutiny, he could only take home a male or spayed female and never more than two. Perry became the sole breeder of the Chinook dog and would not reveal its origin.

In 1965, the *Guinness Book of World Records* recorded the Chinook for the first time as the "Rarest Dog in the World," with only 125 living and the number dropping rapidly. According to the Chinook Owners Association, by 1981, there were only 11 breedable Chinook dogs in the world. The remaining 11 dogs were divided between Neil and Marra Wollpert in Ohio, Kathy Adams in Maine and Peter Abrahams in California. Many others joined the ranks of breeders, and by 1990, the Chinook population was up to 140.

The Chinook breed was recognized by the United Kennel Club (UKC) in March 1991. It has been registered, and to this date, over four hundred purebred Chinooks are registered with the UKC. The Chinook Owners Association, the national breeding program and Chinook crosses recognized by the program are eligible for Limited Privileges registration with the UKC.

The fact that Perry used in his kennel name the words "Chinook Kennels" caused considerable confusion. It was a natural name choice, as he was the only breeder of Chinook dogs, but it was not the Chinook Kennels that was imbedded in the memory of the public as Rear Admiral Byrd's kennels. After a while, Short Seeley's hackles went up every time she had to go through the lengthy explanation about why her kennels, and not the one in Maine, were those associated with United States Antarctic exploration.

Of course, New Hampshire's Chinook Kennels were AKC connected, while Perry Greene's were not, and people who bought pedigreed show stock did not understand why the dogs they bought from Seeley did not have "of Chinook Kennels" attached to their registered names. Milton and Eva had settled on "Kotzebue" for their malamutes and "Alyeska" for their Siberian bloodlines. This, they felt, identified the type of dogs to a public who did not always know that the Chinook Kennels was not producing only yellow dogs from the Walden lineage. The problem was that the Seeleys' kennels became the foundation of the two sledding breeds they produced, and people wanted their dogs' registered names to reflect the blueblood lines from which they descended. Mrs. Seeley began to add "of Chinook" to her malamute lines. She had already begun to use "of Wonalancet" with some of her Siberian huskies. This worked well for malamute and husky owners who wanted to wear the Chinook connection like a banner, but it was even more confusing to the rest of the public.

The Chinook today is a valued family pet as well as an excellent sled dog. The breed has gained popularity in both obedience and conformation shows and has demonstrated its ability in weight-pulling competitions, recreational sledding, agility, fly ball and even herding. The Chinook is a wonderful all-around dog with an exceptional disposition and undying loyalty to its family.

## CHINOOK AND ARTHUR WALDEN, "THE DRIVER AND HIS DOG"

During the 1930s, Arthur Walden wrote several articles and stories of his early sled dog experiences in the Yukon, at his New Hampshire home at Wonalancet and on his adventures with Admiral Byrd's expedition in the Antarctic with his lead dog, Chinook. Some of these stories appeared in the *Appalachia* publication during the 1940s. In this chapter, I wish to share some of Walden's knowledge of the sled dogs and his lead dog, Chinook.

Chinook was born on January 17, 1917, in a litter of golden puppies at Walden's Wonalancet Farm. In March 1926, Arthur Walden, Chinook and his team were the first to ascend Mount Washington by dog sled.

In 1927, Walden heard of the Byrd Expedition to the Antarctic, whereupon he traveled to Boston to meet the admiral and offer his services for the expedition. Admiral Byrd appointed him as chief of the dog teams for the trip.

Admiral Byrd wrote in *Little America*:

> *Had it not been for the dogs, our attempts to conquer the Antarctic by air must have ended in failure. On January 17th, Walden's single team of thirteen dogs moves 3,500 pounds of supplies from ship to base, a distance of 16 miles each trip, in two journeys. Walden's team was the backbone of our transport. Seeing him rush his heavy loads along the trail, outstripping the younger men, it was difficult to believe that he was an old man. He was 58 years old, but he had the determination and strength of youth.*

During the expedition, on Chinook's twelfth birthday, the lead dog wandered away from the camp and was never found. Arthur Walden had lost his best friend. Admiral Byrd wrote:

# A History of Dog Sledding in New England

Arthur Walden and his lead sled dog, Chinook, of Wonalancet, New Hampshire. This pose was announcing the Quebec International Sled Dog Race in 1922. Arthur Walden trained and raced his dogs in both Wonalancet and at the Chinook Kennels, which became a feature attraction throughout New England. At the small Wonalancet Kennels, which specialized in Chinook dogs, Mr. and Mrs. Arthur T. Walden maintained the facility. Here at the kennels was Admiral Byrd's own team of seven dogs, all born at Little America. Arthur Walden accompanied Admiral Byrd to the Antarctic in the 1920s.

## Chinook

> *The second incident, perhaps the saddest during our whole stay in the Antarctic, was the loss of Walden's famous lead dog, Chinook. Chinook was Walden's pride, and there was no doubting the fact that he was a great dog. He was old when brought to the Antarctic, too old for hard, continuous labor, and Walden used him as a kind of "shock troop," throwing him into a team when the going turned very hard. Then the gallant heart of the old dog would rise above the years and pull with the glorious strength of a three-year-old, perhaps the saddest* [incident] *during our whole stay in Antarctica.*

Needless to say, the news of Chinook's death was heard around the world, for his fame as a sled dog leader was highly publicized. If you were to go to the small town of Wonalancet, New Hampshire, you would find that Route 113A from Tamworth to Wonalancet still bears the name "The Chinook Trail" in his memory.

## *"The Driver and His Dog"*

## *February 1925*

In the year 1925, the *Boston Sunday Post* announced that Chinook would be running his "last race," the Fourth Eastern International Sled Dog Derby. "Every dog team had to have a good lead dog if he expected to get anywhere," explained Arthur Walden. "A good lead dog should have about the same qualities of leadership as a leader of men. The best dogs for freight hauling purposes," he continued, "were obtained by crossbreeding the native Eskimo dog with some large domesticated dog, like the St. Bernard, boarhound or mastiff."

Chinook, Arthur Walden's lead dog, tells an unusual and interesting story of the local race, which took place in 1925, when all of New England was looking to Walden and his lead dog to take the trophies. Listen to Chinook as he tells of his adventure:

> *Well friend, it is the Fourth Eastern International Sled Dog Derby, and I'm going to be in it from start to finish.*
>
> *My master, Arthur T. Walden of Wonalancet, is depending on me to lead his gang hitch to victory, and I'm going to do my best to bring home the bacon.*
>
> *Newspapers throughout the country have barked about me as being the "world's super sled dog." That's some reputation, considering the heroic*

service to humanity rendered by Kason's "Balto" and Seppala's "Scotty" in saving stricken Nome, Alaska, and I realize that I must convince my admirers that they haven't been barking up the wrong tree.

What's more important to me, as it would be to any dog for that matter, is the pleasing of my master. He is known and recognized as an able breeder, trainer and driver of sled dogs in the East, if not the best in the country, and I must not fail his, or my loving mistress either, in this, my last great race.

I didn't mean to let that last secret leak out, but you can put it down. Chinook will run his last race. Yes, it will be my farewell appearance in the harness in competition and I'm just quivering with enthusiasm, matching my wits, skill and strength with the best of' them.

"You are a family dog now, Chinook," he told me the other day, "and you must settle down. No more of this sporting life for you, which drains the energy you should give to your children, if you would have them be worthy of their sire."

My lord has spoken, and his word to me is law.

Much as I felt like howling out a protest against retirement from the sport of red-blooded men and dogs, now becoming so popular in New England, I held my tongue. Gracefully, as becomes a dog, I will be obedient to my master's command. It would be base ingratitude, after all he has done for me, to do otherwise.

My age, of course, has much to do with my master's decision as to my future. I'm nine, which corresponds to about the human age of forty. That's pretty old for an athlete, I'll admit, but occasionally the "ol' timer" in the sporting world come through with a brilliant victory when they are looked upon as "has-beens."

It took Stenroos of Finland, age forty-three, to win the grueling marathon grind at the Olympic games, and Walter Johnson to make Washington first in the American League, as well as in peace and war, and then a "World's Champion."

True, like them, I'm not as young as I used to be. When a youngster, I loved to sleep out on the snow on the coldest winter night, but now I prefer to snooze indoors. I shiver now-a-day as the wintry morning air penetrates my coat, and I have to shake a kink or two out of my legs occasionally.

Once I'm in the harness, I'm all right, as I heard a New Hampshire farmer say to one of his pretty young lady boarders from Boston last summer.

You see, age and experience have taught me to use my head and save my feet, to conserve my strength for greater emergencies. In this coming race I *mean to draw on all my cunning, use every brain I've got, pull every trick of the trade I know within the bounds of good sportsmanship, in order to win.*

*My master has groomed me for the race as he never did before, and he wouldn't think of driving me in a hard race if I showed the least indication of being lame or sore.*

*I know that he wants me to end my racing career in a blaze of glory, but I feel confident of making the grade. I'm down to 104 pounds in weight, my mind is perfect, my feet and muscles hard and I never felt better in my life. Only the other night I gave my master the fastest ride he has ever had, I heard him say as much to Mr. Calvert, the Secretary of the New England Sled Dog Club, the other night, and tell him to be sure and record the incident in the annals of the organization.*

*I had my muzzle laid across his boots and my eyes closed as he talked; he thought I was snoozing. I heard it all and it was an effort for me to keep from whooping with delight and impolitely interrupting the narrative:*

"In all my experience driving dog teams," Arthur Walden related, "I never had such a speedy ride behind them as I did going back to my farm at Wonalancet from the carnival at Meredith."

Arthur Walden continued:

*As we approached Center Harbor, the whole outfit was just jogging along taking it easy, but all of a sudden the sled was almost jerked out from under me. Both feet slipped off the runners, but I managed to cling to the handlebars and get my footing again.*

*By this time every dog in the hitch, following Chinook's lead, was at full gallop. They were barely flying over the snow, and crouched over the sled, with my head down to shield my face from the biting wind, I went through Center Harbor so fast that I didn't even see the town.*

*What could have gotten into these dogs, I wondered as they kept up their terrific pace. They've either suddenly realized that they're hungry and homeward bound, or that the devil himself is at their heels. I didn't know how they could have come to that conclusion, for I don't believe in using the lash on them.*

*I soon learned the cause of their extraordinary burst of speed, when they all came to an abrupt halt and performed a chorus of growls and yelps that fairly rent the evening air.*

*"What's up Chinook?" I said, and I looked in the direction in which he had turned. What do you suppose I saw? A black cat was up a tree by the*

side of the road, and there were tracks in the snow showing she had jumped out of the path of my dogs to safety. She had evidently been just a leap or two ahead of Chinook for a mile or more and dared not jump on either side for fear the dogs would pounce on her before she could reach a tree. It took some time to get the minds of my pups off the cat and the harness untangled, but I finally got them started, and they went right along home at their regular pace.

## *Derby Time*

The following is an account of the 1925 Laconia race.

> This year the classic will be even harder than before with a dozen seasoned drivers and the cream of the sled dogs from both Canada and the United States taking part. Brydges is coming on to try to repeat his victory of '24; and from Le Pas also Shorty Russick, winner of last year's 200-mile race there and Bill Grayson, who won La Pas race three years in succession, are scheduled to appear.
>
> Chinook knew he had the best team and that behind him in the harness was good red blood, for all his teammates were his own sons and daughters. There was "Kaltag," "Trontak," "Jules," the leader of the team driven very successfully by Caryl Peabody of Cambridge in several carnival races; and "Sallei," "Skagwa," and "Kaggaruk." Chinook also knew that behind him was a driver who knew the game and would get the best there was from the team without resorting to the whip.
>
> The occasion was the first of the three 41 mile laps of the International Sled Dog Derby, and Emile St. Godard's Manitoba huskies streaked it in four hours and six minutes. It wasn't much of a licking that our best dog team took; however, for although eight Canadian outfits breezed across the finish line before Arthur Walden, the first of the Americans brought his beauties home. Walden's actual running time was less than 40 minutes behind the leader, and with two more days to go, and his dogs in perfect condition, the American veteran was confident that he would chisel down the Canadian lead.
>
> In 1924, a 16 year old, Earl Brydges, came on with a team from Manitoba and was allowed to compete. He was only a wisp of a lad, but he ran the field deaf, dumb and blind in the three days' mushing and carried home a gold cup and $1,000 in cash. This year he came back, and with him came the three best drivers in all Western Canada—all native Manitobans and champions.

# Chinook

*They asked to enter and after deliberation, the committee decided to grant the request, for the annual Derby—the committee wisely decided they might as well throw it open to the world.*

*It was the first time these Manitobans have matched dogs with the Easterners and the Yankees. They are fine fellows, these Manitobans; gaunt Scotty McDonald—fiery little Shorty Russick; silent Emile St. Godard, and the quaint little half-pint Earl Brydges; a fine fellow and excellent sportsmen.*

*Their dogs were unlike any that New England has ever seen. They were hybrid masterpieces of canine breeding with pure Labrador husky as basic strain, crossed through three generations with Russian Wolfhounds and Pointers. The husky blood gave them stamina and strength, the Wolfhound gave them long legs and lean flanks, while the Pointer gave them intelligence.*

*Three of their teams finished one, two, three today, and the fourth was running well up with the leaders until it collided with a log sixteen miles from the finish, smashed its harness and crippled its wheel dog.*

*Their time was the fastest in race history. St. Goddard, the winner, whizzing the 41 mile in 4:06; Earl Brydges HI 4: 13, and Shorty Russick in an even 4:19. No other team was able to break 4:20 and Walden's time 4:43.*

*An even twenty-two teams reported to Judge Souther and Mooney at 9:00 am to the start on the ice below the Mill Bridge. The whole valley was massed about the starters. Beautiful maidens in flaming sports costumes, tourists, portly businessmen from the city and chattering housewives were all part of the variegated background.*

*Underfoot, conditions were ideal for the runners, but the day was too warm. The air was alive with the baying of one hundred and fifty-three dogs, hitched usually seven to a sled. The drivers had trouble holding them as they waited their starting turns, for they lunged ever and again toward the shimmering trail, whining and snarling with impatience to get moving.*

*At three minute intervals they were sent away. Only one bad smashup was featured at the start. This occurred when Al Robert's dogs, seven powerful mongrels, dumped him into the snow, as if by a pre-arranged signal, and charged madly into the Vachter team as it drew up to the line as first starter.*

*In a fierce five-minute fight, which was all whirling fur, gleaming fangs and froth flecked with blood, both teams were wrecked and two of Robert's dogs were so badly cut that they had to be sent back to the stables.*

*The teams were eventually untangled and started on schedule time, although Roberts, of course, had only five dogs.*

# A History of Dog Sledding in New England

*The route was a forty-one mile triangle, striking straight north for sixteen miles, doubling back approximately nine miles to the southwest, then cutting back across the lake some sixteen miles to the finish. It was packed with virgin snow, and since a light sticky snow started falling at mid-morning and continued all through the day, the approximate ten minutes an hour time of the leaders was considered to be truly remarkable.*

*The feature of the first fifteen miles was the strong fight of Alan Robert's team. With only five dogs, he passed the Vachter team and held the lead until one of his five went lame and had to be loaded aboard the sled. One by one after that, the others poured past him and he finished fifth in the list, practically out of it for another day.*

*The real feature of the day, to those who love dogs and intelligent "dogmanship," was provided by the veteran Arthur Walden, Dean of the American competitors. The Squire of Wonalancet was driving the most peculiar team in the contest; led by his famous Chinook. The wonder dog, however, was more than nine years old. His whiskers were gray as an old man's, and he looked even so much wiser than most old men.*

*But his sons hitched in behind him, were tender youngsters not yet two years old.*

*This was their first race, their first crowd, their first competitive dog teams. It was all new and strange and somewhat alarming. But with the broad back of their wise old daddy ahead of them, and the familiar voice of the beloved master behind them, they stepped out when their turn came like six little champions, and struck for the open country with their fuzzy tails flying and their pink tongues lolling.*

*All went well for some sixteen miles, then they began to get tired. For some mysterious reason, they all got frightened, and their fright became a panic. They tried to bolt, tried to wrench themselves free from the harness; they began to cry like frightened children, and not even the disgusted barks of their stern old daddy, who immediately tried to take command of the situation like the shrewd old general that he was, had the slightest effect.*

*Progress was stopped, the sled was almost wrecked, the team was yards off the road and buried in snow before Walden could dismount and reach their heads.*

*Almost any other musher, who ever pushed a sled handle, would have unfolded his whip and handled this insubordination in the good old-fashioned way.*

*Old Arthur Walden was one driver who never used the bat. What he did in this emergency was wholly characteristic of an old-timer who loved his dogs like he loved his family.*

# Chinook

*"Lie down, babies,"* he crooned away out there in the snow, *"we won't run anymore if you don't want to. I know it's hard going, this snow's pretty heavy. Never you mind, there's nothing to worry about. There's nothing to get scared of. There comes a fellow passing us, but we don't care."*

One by one he took their heads in his lap and stroked and talked to them as if they understood. He told them that they were the finest dogs that any man ever drove and that he was mighty proud of every one of them.

Gradually, the whining stopped and the trembling and stage fright passed. Old Chinook was talking to them, too, barked gruffly, but not too gruffly.

Finally, Walden stood up. So did the dogs. Chinook gave a couple of canine commands. They all leaped into the collar. Walden righted the overturned sled, and they yanked it back onto the trail.

From there on they teamed it like champions. They came home with their tails flying valiantly and licked Walden's hand when he unharnessed them at the stable, They finished in much better shape than any of the other dogs in the race, but Walden had lost a precious half-hour out there on the trail. That's a half-hour that will never be totally made up. Walden loses the race by a close margin.

# V
# THE SLED DOG

Seeing the teams bolt over the trails in the weekend sled dog races throughout New England, spectators have expressed confusion about the genus of sled dog. They have seen big dogs, little dogs, heavy dogs, light dogs, wolfhounds and even Irish setters and coonhounds running the same courses in the race against time. The only common denominator is that they are dogs, and to make the unique sport of sled dog racing more pleasurable for the spectators, the following is an endeavor to provide an understanding of just what is a sled dog.

Sled dogs are expected to demonstrate their physical capability to pull a sled. Their endurance is necessary to travel the distance demanded of them. Speed is needed to travel the distance in some reasonable length of time.

The dogs may pull various types of sleds, from the small, twenty-five-pound sprint-racing sleds through the larger, plastic-bottomed distance racing toboggan sleds to the traditional ash freighting sleds. Sled dogs are also used to pull kick sleds and to draw wheeled rigs when there is no snow. The modern teams are usually hitched in tandem, with harnessed pairs of sled dogs pulling on tug lines attached to a central gang line. Dog teams of some Inuits are run in a "fan hitch," each dog having its own towline directly to the sled.

## Would You Like to Race a Dog Team?

*Cynthia Molburg provided the following article, as published in the* Derby '74 *by the Lakes Region Sled Dog Club.*

Dogs are a lot like people, maybe not as intelligent (and that's a point of view of the non-dog person), but still a lot like people. Unlike horse racing, the driver of a team has to put a whole group of "individuals" together, and that does create some intriguing challenges in that the driver is attempting to make "several" dogs react to his or her desires as a "single" animal, as a "team."

The dogs that are seen at any sled dog racing classics are the result of long hours of training and communication. The leaders have learned to take commands from the driver, and most of the time this is automatic, but once in a while a set of circumstances, and a resulting lack of response, will create havoc. That's one of those frustrating times.

But—there is no way to describe the exhilaration granted only to the "dog man" when his or her team moves swiftly over the trail in unison, the silence being broken only by the whisper of the sled runners. Sled dog racing is unique in that it is a sport where one driver challenges another and one dog team is pitted against another, but there are times during the race when the driver senses a feeling of "being alone with the team"—the other competitors and spectators fade away in the lonely, wooded sections of the trail.

When the lead dog strains and jumps in harness to leave the starting line and the crowds, his/her teammates and the driver are headed into a world only known to those who take up the challenge of sled dog racing.

So—you'd like to race a dog team? If you are patient, understanding and have a longing for a very personal relationship with dogs and nature, you really should look into it!

## Spectator Tips

After reading through this book and having grown an understanding of the sled dog racing sport, you might want to cheer for and let the driver know you appreciate his or her team's effort. As in all sports, it's nice to know you have someone cheering you on. I have my favorites (maybe that's obvious!).

Feel free to visit the holding area and take all the pictures you want. Be careful where you walk, for there are many things to trip over, such as chains, sleds, harnesses, etc. Ask the driver questions if he or she is not busy. Most dog people love to talk about their dogs; however, getting a team ready to go takes a lot of work, and at times they may not be able to talk.

NEVER bring a dog or cat to a sled dog race. If you do, leave it in your car. A driver handling several dogs cannot be responsible for your pets. There have been races lost and pets injured because a team swerved off the trail after a stray dog or cat.

These dogs are trained racing dogs. You should never feed or offer them anything without the permission of the driver. As a rule, sled dogs are very friendly; however, do not pet them without first checking with the driver. NEVER tease the dogs.

Take all the pictures you want but keep in mind the following things. If you use a flash, please use it with discretion. A race was lost because a photographer flashed in front of a team, causing them to spook while streaking for the finish line. The second place team passed by, winning because of this incident.

Finally, if you are near the starting line or on the trail, please stand back, as anyone too close may distract the dogs and even cause them to leave the trail. It is also much easier if the crowd is not all jammed together. Please enjoy the race!

## The Sled Dog Racing Breeds and Musher's Vocabulary

### By Dick Moulton

Mushers speak a colorful dialect of their own that, except for a few of the more spicy phrases, may be confusing to the novice spectator of sled dog races. Knowing a few of the terms and commands that are used makes watching a sled dog race all the more interesting.

**Alaskan husky**: a term that applies to dogs originating from Alaska, also called Indian and Eskimo dogs.
**Alaskan malamute**: Probably the oldest breed of sled dog, used more for freighting than racing because of its large size and weight, which can reach one hundred pounds. This type of dog was originally bred as an Alaskan sled dog.
**all right, let's go**: commands to move forward. These vary depending on the musher; however, "mush" is rarely used for this command.

# A History of Dog Sledding in New England

A typical Siberian husky sled dog. *Photo by Bernice Perry.*

**Chinook**: a rare New England sled dog breed of "in-between" type, neither a sprinter nor endurance freighter. The original lead dog Chinook, on whom the breed is based, was a mixture of working sled dog lines of a mastiff-type build. The breed varies in appearance much more than most sled dog breeds and often resembles a yellow German shepherd mix.

**come gee or come haw**: commands to turn around and reverse direction to right or left.

**Eskimo husky**: larger than the Siberian husky and not generally used for racing except by Alaskan Eskimos. It is often a cross of several northern dogs.

# The Sled Dog

**gee**: turn right.
**haw**: turn left.
**husky**: a term that is generally applied to all northern breeds of dogs.
**Irish setter**: not commonly thought of as a sled dog, but these dogs are very fast under certain conditions.
**musher**: a sled dog driver.
**mushing**: a general term used for the sport powered by dogs, which includes sled dog racing. Specifically, it implies the use of one or more dogs to pull a sled on snow. This term is used as a command—to go, commence pulling is "mush."
**pedaling**: the driver keeps one foot on the runner of the sled while pushing with the other.
**Quebec hound**: a term used for dogs originating from Quebec, Canada. They may be a cross of various hound breeds, German shepherds and huskies.
**Samoyed**: a pure or mostly white Spitz that was used for herding reindeer as well as pulling sleds.
**Seppala**: this Siberian sled dog is active and energetic, sharing the same ancestral base as the Siberian husky.
**Siberian husky**: a smaller dog, forty to fifty-five pounds, that was brought to Alaska from Siberia at the turn of the century.
**snowball**: snow that collects in a dog's feet while running.
**stoved**: a dog that may be lame or does not feel well.
**towline or gang line**: the main line to which all dogs are attached.
**trail**: request by one musher to another for the right of way on the trail when one musher wishes to pass another.

Kingkok, "King of the Sled Dogs," at Ed Clark's Eskimo Sled Dog Ranch in the White Mountains.

# A History of Dog Sledding in New England

Spike Bicknell with her team of four huskies.

**Walker treeing coonhounds**: These dogs have been used very successfully for racing by Don Blodgett of Maine.
**whoa**: command to stop.

The Sled Dog

## A History of Sled Dog Breeds

*Excerpts from this article, "Sled Dogs—It Takes All Kinds," were written by Roger Heath for the* Derby '74, *published by the Lakes Region Sled Dog Club.*

There is an old saying that "every dog has his day." This applies also to the various breeds of dogs, and at the present time, the useful sled dog is having his day in popular esteem, especially throughout the East, due to a large measure of interest aroused by these dogs through the various long-distance sled dog races that have taken place during the past seven years.

The dogs that stand harnessed in front of today's dog sled may be any breed that chance has given some of the specialties for the job. The principal breeds of dogs suitable for useful sled dogs—that is, dogs with sufficient coats to withstand severe cold, with good feet for traveling over snow and ice and with the proper conformation for hauling loaded sleds—are the Siberians, Alaskan malamutes, Russian Samoyeds and Baffin-land, Greenland and Labrador Eskimos.

Roger Heath notes:

> *In the racing dog, the engine is the heart and lungs. They power the mechanical parts, the legs and the shoulders, into motion and carry the frame that holds it together down the trail in a way often more beautiful than efficient, but generally a touch of both.*
>
> *The problem is simply mechanical. In going from the small dog to the very large, the proportion of that dog devoted to the power plant increases less rapidly than that portion devoted to the frame. Thus the large dog may have half again the reach and size of the small dog, but he has only a third more heart and lung capacity to push around twice as much frame.*
>
> *However, more important things than size make that one in five hundred huskies the outstanding animal that pulls team and driver across the line to victories in Anchorage, Fairbanks, St. Paul, and the grueling miles of Laconia, New Hampshire. Proportion means everything. The body must have a length sufficient to give it the stretch and stride that reduces the number of steps in a mile. The legs must be long enough to maintain the stride that the length of the body insists on. The frame must have bulk and substance or it will literally rattle itself into substandard performance. Without enough muscle and bone, the energy is not transferred to the ground efficiently, but is lost on the way in a struggle to keep things together.*

## A History of Dog Sledding in New England

The racing husky that nearly always dominates the race course from Alaska to Quebec and New England is a mixture of blood that takes its heart and good looks from an early Siberian, its speed and build from the Alaskan village dog and its personalized finer point from that kennel down the road that had the dog that had almost everything the dog up the road needed.

The Siberians, which were first imported to Alaska from the Kamchatkan Peninsula and the Boreal Lena River in Siberia, are short-legged dogs with plumed tails. They have a peculiar bounding lope due to the abnormal length of the humorous bone, giving them a powerful, straight-ahead, trail-covering reach. They have short, blocky bodies, are powerful pullers and have great endurance. Like many breeds of dogs, which have been for many generations closely associated with man and are far removed from their wolf ancestors, the Siberians have a sunny, genial disposition and dwell amiably together. These dogs have made some remarkable speed records, especially on hard, wind-packed trails such as are found along the coast sections of Alaska. They hold the record in the 408-mile All-Alaska Sweepstakes of seventy-four hours, fourteen minutes and twenty-two seconds, the total time elapsed between the time of the start at Nome and the return, including all time used for rest en route.

In the Samoyed, we find a breed in many respects similar to the Siberians, as they are dogs that, for many hundreds of years, have been bred and used for sled dogs and as herders of reindeer by the Samoyed people, a nomadic tribe of Finnic origin, inhabiting the Yalmal or Samoyed Peninsula, a vast stretch of tundra that extends along the shores of the Arctic Ocean from the White Sea to the Yenesei River. They are either pure white or biscuit in color. The rigorous climate of his native land makes the Samoyed a dog of activity, strength and toughness, and for his size and weight, he has no equal as a sled dog. Large numbers of these dogs were used in Arctic and Antarctic expeditions, notably those of Nansen, Shackleton, Johannsen, the Duc de'Abruzzi and Borchgrebink, having been found more reliable than the Eskimo, friendly with one another and their masters and with a disposition to work at all times. Shackleton reports that eight Samoyed dogs, averaging only forty pounds each, hauled a sled loaded with eight hundred pounds and two men forty miles in one day, from 7:00 a.m. to 6:00 p.m., with an hour for lunch and a rest of five minutes at regular intervals.

The Eskimos, while not as gentle as the Samoyeds, make fair pets and, being larger, work admirably in harness and are a most useful and desirable type of sled dog.

The North Greenland Eskimo dog is seldom seen out of his natural habitat, but some were placed on exhibition in British Zoos following expeditions in

# The Sled Dog

that area. Descendants of these dogs mixed with the blood of others have appeared in the United States. Admiral Robert E. Peary said of the breed that if it had not been for them, the expedition could not have reached the North Pole. Speaking of one of his dogs, which he later gave to Sir Winfred Grenfell, an English doctor working in Labrador, Peary said, "Polaris is extremely affectionate and gentle with people but a devil incarnate with everything else that walks, swims or flies!" Polaris is said to have celebrated his arrival in Labrador by whipping every other dog in sight.

The Indian dog is frequently confused with the Alaskan husky. They share a common ancestry. Today's breeders have felt fewer bounds in the breeding of this particular racing strain. Whereas the Alaskan husky is usually confined to crossbreeding among the Arctic strains, the Indian dog carries a great variety of bloodlines. As a result, he does not necessarily show the outward characteristics of the Arctic dog, though he may, and he may even show the dominant features of dogs native to the warmer climates. They are generally smaller and lighter than the Alaskan husky but are bred for the same purposes: speed and endurance.

In the huskies, malamutes and breeds that contain a certain amount of wolf blood, we find dogs that are not as reliable as the Siberian, Samoyed and Eskimo, the degree of unreliability being increased with the amount of wolf blood they have. In breeding this type of dog, the aim should be to breed away from the wolf as much as possible, retaining only enough wolf blood to give the huskies the ability to withstand severe climates and the good bone and heavy coat inherited from the wolf. These dogs rarely bark but are great howlers, especially when they are tied up. They make a good dog for heavy hauling, weighing from eighty to one hundred pounds, with wide shoulders and well-sprung ribs, and a team of five dogs is capable of hauling seventy-five to one hundred pounds per dog twenty to thirty miles a day. If given a lighter load, they are able to travel twice as far.

The Alaskan malamute is among the oldest of the Arctic dogs, with a history dating back to 1000 BC or earlier. He was named after the Inuit tribe called Malamutes who settled on the shores of Kotzebue Sound in the upper western part of Alaska. Russian explorers were among the first white men to record the malamute's existence. Due to racing interest—the desire for faster dogs—outside blood was introduced into this breed, causing a decay of the Arctic sledge dogs. In 1926, while interest ran high in the Byrd expedition, United States breeders effected the return of the purebred. The malamute is cousin to the Samoyed of Russia, Siberian husky (Kolyma River region) and the Eskimo dogs of Greenland and Labrador. They may weigh from fifty to eighty-five pounds and are powerful and substantially built, with deep chests and a strong, compact bodies. They stand from twenty-three to twenty-five inches tall. Their coat, which may be almost any color but is usually wolfish gray or black and white, consists of a dense wooly undercoat from one to two inches in depth with an outer coat of thick, coarse guard hair. The malamute has a broad head with wedge-shaped ears, a bulky muzzle and brown, almond-shaped eyes. Mask or cap markings are very common, and the neck is strong and moderately arched. His legs are heavy boned and muscled, and he carries his tail over his back, but not tightly curled like the wolf bush.

Whereas the previously mentioned dogs are members of the working group, sled dog racing, as previously mentioned, is not confined to that particular class, and members of the sporting group are strong contenders in many major racing events.

Irish setters are used on the East and West Coasts of America and Alaska. The setters are relative newcomers to the "Dogdom," dating back to the 1700s in Ireland. The setters are thought to be a probable cross between the English setter, spaniel, pointer and Gordon setter. The red dog of Erin is the lightest of the setter group and the most finely drawn. His "devil-may-care" attitude has been a source of consternation to hunters training him to point and set birds, but it has also caused this breed to become great favorites as companions, and they rarely go "sour" when corrected in training. The fact that they are higher strung than either the Gordon or English setters and are equipped with the best feet and running gear most likely adds to their ability as racing sled dogs. Aristocratic in appearance, weighing in the vicinity of sixty or seventy pounds, with a flat, silky coat that is a rich mahogany color, the Irish setter stands over two feet tall at the shoulders. A long, lean head with a raised brow and delicate chiseling of the muzzle around and below the eyes and along the cheek adds to the setter's beauty. The eyes are somewhat almond shaped, dark and medium brown, with a soft, alert expression. The ears are well set back, hanging in a neat fold close to the head and nearly long enough to touch the nose. The deep chest, sturdy legs and sufficiently long body of the setter permits a free stride when the dog is in motion. The feet are well feathered, and the tail has longer hair, which is commonly called a "flag."

Coonhounds have taken to the sled dog trails in recent years and add a comic touch to the race with their baying as though in pursuit. These dogs are said to be descendants of the Talbot hound, which was known in England during the reign of William I, duke of Normandy, in the eleventh century. Hence, their ancestry runs down through the bloodhound and foxhound until today's coonhound emerged. There are several different variations in the breed, which includes different types of markings and colors, but through selective breeding, the black and tan coonhound has gained recognition in the kennel clubs. These dogs average between twenty-three and twenty-five inches in height and have straight forelegs and cat-like feet. Their hindquarters are well boned and muscled, enabling them to run easily for a long distance, which is often required of them during a hunt. They have a short, dense coat and muscular neck and carry their tail freely. The coonhound's eyes are hazel to dark brown in color, and the ears are set low and well back, hanging in a graceful fold.

Other breeds are used in both the pure and mixed forms on the sled dog teams. Among them are the Labrador retriever, English setter in the sporting class; the greyhound and whippet of the hound class and the collie, Doberman pinscher and German shepherd of the working class.

These are the popular breeds, classes and mixes of the dog in this sport. So it goes, with each new winter and every race, the quest for a perfect racing dog continues ad infinitum.

Many sled dog races that have been run in the West and East have brought out the special qualifications of the various breeds. The long-distance nonstop races, such as the 408-mile All-Alaska Sweepstakes, have now given way to the lap races, such as are run from Quebec. These races serve a practical purpose, provided only the proper type of useful sled dog is allowed to enter—dogs with good feet, coat and proper conformation for hauling sleds. With such dogs competing under conditions that approximate actual working conditions where they are used by explorers, miners, mail carriers, etc., these races serve to greatly stimulate an interest in the proper breeding of a useful type of sled dog.

As Roger Heath notes:

> *It should be remembered that the sled dog, like the sled, is the evolution of things once meant for another purpose, but it claims a longer struggle to the purpose at hand than almost all but man him or herself. The result in its increasing performance make the sport and the animal among the most visible and beautiful thing on the landscape today and certainly the finest of sights on the winter trails.*

## Dog Team Members

Dog team members are given titles according to their positions in the team relative to the sled. These include the leaders (lead dog), swing dogs, team dogs and wheelers or wheel dogs.

## A History of Dog Sledding in New England

World champion sled dog racer Harris Dunlap, of Bakers Mills, New York, inspects his team with the aid of his wife, Ginger (kneeling), before the start of competition. "Musher marriages" are increasingly common in sled dog racing, with husbands and wives competing in different events. More than one hundred dog teams were expected to run in the $30,000 ALPO International Sled Dog Championships, January 27–29, 1984, in Saranac Lake, New York. *Photo by Don Hyman.*

**lead dog(s)**: steers the rest of the team and sets the pace. Leaders may be single or double. Qualities for a good lead dog are intelligence, enthusiasm, common sense and the ability to find a trail in bad weather.

**swing dogs (or point dogs)**: are directly behind the leader. They direct the rest of the team behind them in turns or curves on the trail. (Some mushers use the term swing dog to denote a team dog.)

# The Sled Dog

**team dogs**: those between the wheelers and the point dogs, adding power to the team. A small team may not have dogs in this position.
**wheel dogs**: those nearest the sled; a good wheeler must have a relatively calm temperament so as not to be startled by the sled moving just behind it. Strength, steadiness and ability to help guide the sled around tight curves are qualities valued in "wheelers."

## SLED DOG RACING— AN INTERNATIONAL SPORT

*Cynthia Molburg, publisher of* Team & Trail, *has provided the following article, which appeared in the* Derby 74 *annual publication of the Lakes Region Sled Dog Club.*

Over the past few years, and as a result of improved communication, sled dog racing has become an international sport. It was only a short time ago that race areas and race-sponsoring organizations were isolated from one another, and people in New England raced under one set of rules, Alaskans under another, Canadians under another and so on. To a small extent, this situation still exists today, but with better communication, and following the formation of the International Sled Dog Racing Association (ISDRA) in 1966, uniformity of race rules and race procedure is emerging to the fore of the racing scene. ISDRA is composed of representatives from all over the racing world, including European countries, Canada and the United States.

At one time, the major "racing classics" could be counted on one hand—those that existed in Alaska, the Quebec City Dog Derby, the La Pas, Manitoba race and the Laconia World Championship Sled Dog Derby. The year 1969 saw the beginning of the Midwest racing circuit when the St. Paul Winter Carnival introduced the East Meets West Race, which included drivers from both the East and West Coasts of the United States and teams from Canada. Today, Ely, Minnesota's All American Championship and Kaalkaska, Michigan's Midwest Championship are attracting top mushers from all over the North American continent, just as is being done in Quebec, Laconia and Alaska.

In 1974, a "western racing circuit" has become quite influential, having been instigated by the successful Priest Lake, Idaho, and Jackson Hole, Wyoming races. Easterners are beginning to travel to the far west as a result of the attractive purses and a desire to challenge the western driver who can point with pride to the fact that one of the oldest, if not *the* oldest, "lower forty-eight" races was run in his country, the 1917 Ashton, Idaho American Dog Derby.

As a result of ISDRA and the import of Siberian huskies to the European countries from the States, American-style sled dog racing has been introduced to Switzerland, Germany, Finland and Norway. Even though Holland can boast of a few teams, a law that prohibits the use of dogs as draft animals has curbed racing activity in the country.

But a "sled dog sport" did exist in northern Europe prior to the introduction of "racing," as it is known on this continent, whereby one, two and three dogs were hitched tandem style to a toboggan-like sled known as a *pulkah*. The pulkah is weighted in proportion to the number of dogs on the team, and the driver travels on skis. Such races are still being run in the Scandinavian countries and are now being considered by drivers on this side of the Atlantic as a competitive activity for the owner of a limited number of dogs.

Sled dog racing is truly going international"!

# FROM NOME TO CANDLE

## *An International Tradition*

*The early history of sled dog racing would be incomplete without mention of the first All Alaskan Sweepstakes race from Nome to Candle and back. Cynthia Molburg provides the following account.*

The records of formal racing events date back to 1908 with the running of the first All-Alaska Sweepstakes race, a distance of 408 miles from Nome to Candle and back. The winning time was turned in by John Hegness, driving a team owned by Albert Fink in 119 hours, 15 minutes and 12 seconds. In 1910, the record for this same trail was reduced to 74 hours, 14 minutes and 37 seconds by John Johnson, driving a team owned by Colonel Ramsey.

Although these races were of import to Alaskans, it was not until 1925 that people outside Alaska's borders took a serious look at sled dogs. It was then that Nome was struck by a diphtheria epidemic, and the lifesaving serum was brought into the stricken city over a distance of 674 miles by relay dog teams and drivers. Among them was Leonhard Seppala, whose 90-mile run to Golovin in minus thirty-degree temperatures and a strong wind that blew off the Bering Sea attracted the attention of the international news media and led him to racing fame in Canada and New England.

Sled dog racing, as a sport, probably got its start in Alaska when a team driver of one village challenged a driver of another. Today, sled dog racing prospers throughout the villages, and notable classics awarding a fine purse of money are run annually in Anchorage and Fairbanks. Many prestigious winners have emerged from these races, with winning team performances averaging up to seventeen miles per hour on the hard-packed and flat trails.

In March 1973, the longest and richest sled dog race in history was held on the historic Iditarod Trail leading into interior Alaska and the gold fields, part of which was used for the Nome Serum Run. It was over one thousand miles long, from Anchorage to Nome, and awarded a total of $50,000 in purse money. Dick Wilmarth, a thirty-year-old miner and bush pilot, won the race with a time of twenty days, forty-nine minutes and forty-one seconds. Wilmarth is a former trapper, and this was his first encounter in a sled dog race.

Hopefully, the Iditarod will run for many years to come, and Anchorage and Fairbanks will be in there vying for the best competition that North America and the world has to offer.

## THE FAMOUS IDITAROD TRAIL

*Based on an account for Iditarod's "Eye on the Trail"*

*Written by Iditarod competitor Jon Little*

Deborah Molburg stamped her name on major sled dog races in the Northeast before moving to Alaska in 1981 with her husband, Sandy Bicknell. There, the dedicated dog driver maintained a kennel in the Yukon, and after giving it some serious consideration, entered the renowned thousand-mile Iditarod Trail Race from Anchorage to Nome in 2007 and 2008. Following is Jon Little's account of the 2008 race:

> *March 18, 2008—The 2008 Iditarod Trail Sled Dog Race was officially over with the arrival of Red Lantern winner, Deborah Bicknell.*
> 
> *Bicknell's eight-dog team trotted under the burled arch about 8:30 p.m. Monday to an enthusiastic crowd of dignitaries and fans. There she blew out the widow's lamp, which is left lit while there's a team still on the trail. It took her 15 days, 5 hours and 36 minutes to complete the trail, almost six days slower than the winner, Lance Mackey. Mackey was among those at the finish line to greet Bicknell.*
> 
> *The second time proved to be a charm for Bicknell, who returned to the Iditarod in 2008 after enduring a 30-hour-long adventure last year*

lost in a blizzard and drenched by a slip in the Kuskokwim River in the heart of the Alaskan Range. This year, Bicknell helped a couple of other mushers—Liz Parrish and Molly Yazwinski—and wound up getting the honor of being the last team across the finish when Yazwinski scratched and Parrish's team surged ahead.

"I was planning on not being last," the 62-year-old daughter of a longtime mushing family, said. "My dog team is better than that."

This is an annual event in that it doesn't really have losers, whether you are first or seventy-eighth as Bicknell was. Eighteen more teams started the race but couldn't make it to Nome for one reason or another. It's true that anyone who finishes the Iditarod has accomplished a feat in itself.

Even with outstanding snow conditions that year, making for a generally smooth trail, the Iditarod is rarely without its hair-raising moments, and it typically dishes out a little extra punishment for those who stay out on the trail longer. 2008 proved no exception. The infamous Solomon Blowhole, only 27 miles from the finish line, was silent for the front runners but roared to life and pummeled the very back of the pack with howling winds and blowing snow. It was the only place that pinned Bicknell down and with Nome practically in sight.

Bicknell lost sight of the trail and spent three hours Monday afternoon sitting in the midst of fierce winds and snow blowing so hard that it buried her curled up dogs. The blowhole is about a five-mile long stretch of innocent looking beach front, but it's at the foot of some treeless hills that form a kind of air funnel from the interior to the shore. It can blow hurricane force from right to left across a trail marked with reflectors set on tripods and upright pieces of driftwood. The fact that it occurs just before the checkpoint called "Safety" is no coincidence.

Bicknell had come up the Topkok Hills from White Mountain only about 45 minutes behind Parrish, who was waiting for her in an emergency cabin just before the blowhole. Parrish thought they should go across together. Bicknell wanted to rest her dogs, which she did. In hindsight, she said she should have teamed up.

Bicknell's leaders had a tough time staying on the trail. They drifted right into the wind then shot left on command, but crossed right over the trail and kept going up a little knoll, Bicknell said. Disoriented and wanting to calm her spooked dogs, she gathered them up in the lee of her overturned sled land and waited and waited.

She was already in last place at this point. Parrish had long since crossed the finish line, so Bicknell waited patiently until a snowmobile driver came along to point the way back to Nome. She caught sight of the trail marker in the direction he pointed, got her dogs lined out and continued on her way.

"It was pretty easy in the end," she said. "I felt like a drama queen, y'know. Last year, the river and this year, the blowhole."

Bicknell would spend Tuesday relaxing and then partake in the second finishers' banquet in the evening, along with other backpack finishers and others still in Nome. The race always holds a banquet for any finisher, and a 15-day red lantern is very respectable. The fastest red lantern finish, David Straub in 2002, was 14 days and 5 hours.

There are many, many races within the race, and this year it became obvious there was a three-woman effort to make it up the trail. Bicknell helped Parrish, who had badly hurt her hip in a fall near Rohn; in turn, Parrish helped Molly Yazwinski, who had to drop her key lead dog by the Yukon River. Yazwinski worked tirelessly to keep her leaderless team moving, and would trail Parrish sometimes so the dogs would chase.

But Yazwinski couldn't get her team to leave White Mountain and had to scratch there, a frustratingly short 77 miles from the end of the race. Before leading out on the trail to Nome, Bicknell told Yazwinski, who had a veterinary school waiting in the wings, she'd have to return in 2009 to finish the job.

Bicknell, who lived in Auke Bay, just outside Juneau, had put off knee surgery to make way for her Iditarod dream, but she felt good physically most of the way. She said she had a "to do" list, and the Iditarod was on it, adding, "This is what I did. I checked it off yesterday."

## SLED DOG TRAILS

*Hard Work and Community Spirit Makes It All Possible*

A tremendous amount of work and cooperation goes into the preparation of a major event like the World Championship Sled Dog Derby. Planning for the annual race is a yearlong task, under the direction of the Lakes Region Sled Dog Club. Critiques of the race are submitted by the drivers to the club officials at the conclusion of each race. These comments from those who complete the race, and the tests of strength and stamina, often form the basis for future improvements in the World Championship Sled Dog Derby.

The board of directors of the Lakes Region Sled Dog Club meets throughout the year to coordinate the details that make the race such a

# A History of Dog Sledding in New England

Making the sled dog trail: Lyman Construction Company of Gilford, New Hampshire.

success. Board officials meet with the landowners, who graciously and generously permit their backyards and pastures to be used for the eighteen-mile trail. During the early fall months, volunteers from the club work to clear brush and other obstacles to ensure a clear trail for the February race. Then, several weeks before each race, a crew headed by the Lyman Construction Company of Gilford, bulldozes and packs the trail, with final checks of the course made just minutes prior to each race.

There is a great deal of work behind the scenes for the sled dog races, but especially for the Laconia race, that often goes unnoticed, such as publicity and securing race sponsors and many, many more details that are necessary to put the whole thing together. Then there is the cooperation and generosity of area businessmen, city officials, police and public works employees to ensure that everything goes smoothly. There is a great deal of work and community spirit that goes into the making of an event such as this. For all who lend a helping hand, the Lakes Region Sled Dog Club wishes to express its sincere thank you!

# The Sled Dog

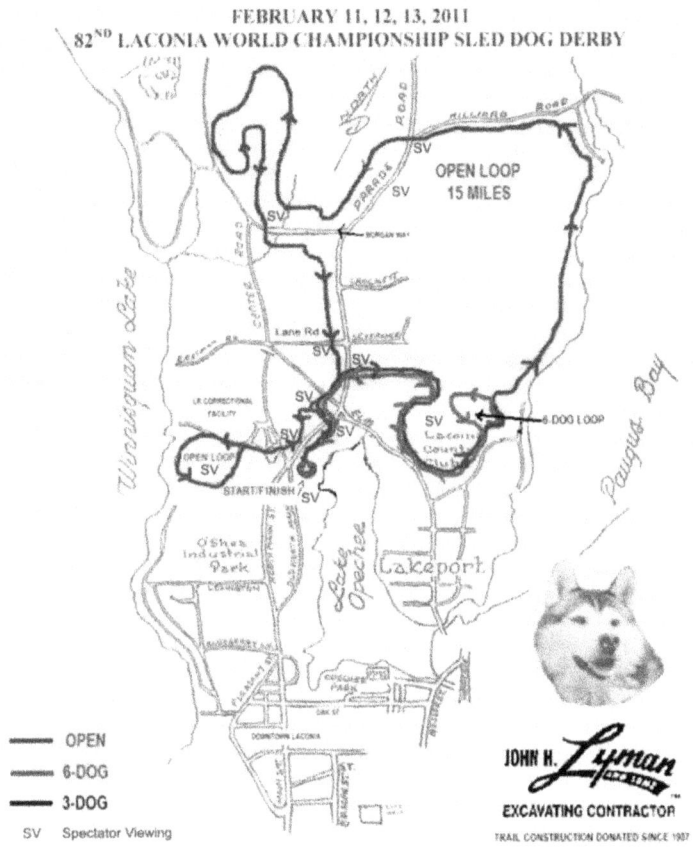

*Above*: The map of the Eighty-second Laconia World Championship Sled Dog Derby, February 2011.

*Below*: This diagram shows the Sled—towline of gang line.

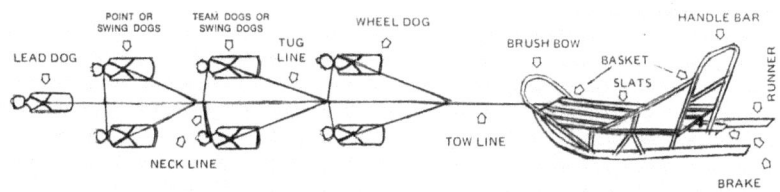

# A History of Dog Sledding in New England

*Above*: Robert Corriveau (#2), 1975 World Championship Sled Dog Race.

*Below*: Laconia's Championship sled dog race, circa 1970s.

# The Sled Dog

*Above*: Two teams racing in Laconia, New Hampshire's championship race, circa 1970s

*Below*: Two dog sleds racing in the 2009 World Championship Derby.

Saranac Lake, New York. Action in the January 27–29 ALPO International Sled Dog Races won't be limited only to the elite mushers with their sixteen-dog unlimited teams. It will also involve assorted small fries, like this three-year-old, who will race their single-dog teams in the popular Kid and Mutt event. The bond between these wonderful animals and their young drivers is one of the most heartwarming aspects of the sport. You're never too young!

# INDEX

## A

Alaska  13, 15, 17, 31, 35, 36, 37, 38, 41, 42, 43, 45, 46, 47, 48, 50, 53, 55, 64, 65, 66, 68, 75, 76, 77, 78, 80, 82, 83, 85, 92, 101, 103, 106, 107, 108, 111, 112, 113
Alaskan malamute  41, 74, 87, 101, 105, 107
Allen, Art  39
Alton Bay  30, 39
Appalachia  89

## B

Bacon, Phil  24, 25
Beland, Don  40
Belford, Charles  8, 43, 73, 82
Bellerive, Claude  8, 44
Belletete, William  16
Benoit, Ed  22
Berlin, NH  13, 14, 32, 33, 34, 56
Berube, Omer  11, 23, 45
Bethlehem, NH  34
Bicknell, Deborah  113, 114, 115
Boissonneault  45
Boscawan, NH  34

Boston, MA  14, 15, 23, 34, 35, 38, 39, 55, 56, 80, 89, 92
breed  13, 17, 22, 61, 63, 68, 71, 77, 78, 79, 80, 85, 86, 88, 89, 92, 95, 101, 102, 103, 105, 106, 107, 108, 109
Bridgewater, NH  34
Bristol, NH  34, 37
Brown Paper Company  14
Brunet, Ernie  39
Bryar, Jean  11, 45, 46, 47, 48, 82, 83, 84
Bryar, Keith II  11, 44, 48, 62
Bryar, Keith Sr.  11, 48, 52, 53, 54, 55, 59, 60, 61, 67
Brydges, Ed  16
Byrd, Admiral Richard  16, 41, 69, 70, 72, 74, 80, 81, 88, 89

## C

Calvert, Claude  14, 23, 24, 93
Carrier, Ovide  52
Center Harbor  30, 33, 35, 39, 45, 47, 48, 71, 81, 82, 93
chamber of commerce  32, 39
Channing, Walter  15, 16, 35, 36

# Index

Chinook 14, 16, 23, 40, 73, 74, 78, 79, 80, 81, 84, 85, 86, 87, 88, 89, 91, 92, 93, 94, 97, 102
Chocorua 31
Clark, Edward 15, 16, 25, 35, 36, 55
Clark, Florence 15, 25, 55, 56, 57, 58, 83
Clarkson 55, 56
Clark's Trading Post 11
collie 55, 58, 109
Concord, NH 25, 34
Corbin, Eugene 40
Cowing, Charlie 23, 24, 25

## D

Dadney, Thomas 38
Daigle, Phillip 52
Davis, Robert 33
DeForest, Charles 14
Dekker, Cynthia 67
Dunlap, Harris 68, 81, 82, 83
Dupuis, Francois 16
Dupuis, Joe 16
Duval, Tate 16

## E

Eastern International 33, 79, 91
Edinger, Gary 40
Enebuske, Clara 15
Erhart, Charles 40
Eskimo 15, 32, 34, 47, 57, 58, 69, 78, 79, 83, 91, 101, 102, 105, 106, 107
Estes, Percy 14, 15, 23, 24, 25, 31

## F

Fairbanks, Alaska 43, 45, 47, 55, 84, 105, 113
Flume 34
Franconia, NH 34
Franklin, NH 34

## G

German shepherd 102, 103, 109
Gilmanton, NH 39
Gordon, Ed 25
Gorham 32, 34, 79
Grayson, William 16, 94
Greyhound 38, 39, 78, 109

## H

Haines, Roger 26, 41, 42
Hayford, Charles J. 32
Hayward, Sam 23
Heath, Roger 105, 109
Hound 41, 42, 63, 68, 84, 103, 108, 109

## I

Iditarod 9, 64, 66, 113, 114, 115
international race 14, 38
Irish setter 60, 61, 68, 99, 103, 108
ISDRA (International Sled Dog Racing Association) 29, 30, 68, 69, 73, 74, 82, 83, 111, 112
Iver Johnson Sporting Goods Company 39

## J

Jefferson, NH 34
Johnson, Neal 40
junior drivers 17, 19

## L

Label, Jean 13
Laconia Evening Citizen 11, 36, 63
Laconia, NH 16, 18, 21, 22, 30, 31, 32, 33, 35, 37, 38, 39, 45, 50, 51, 52, 53, 55, 58, 62, 64, 67, 68, 69, 81, 105
Laconia World Championship Sled Dog Derby 14, 31, 43, 60, 63, 64, 72, 78, 82, 83, 84, 111
Lady Mushers 83
Lake Paugus 39
Lake Placid, NY 33, 38, 40, 41, 84
Lakeport, NH 39
Lakes Region Sled Dog Club 22, 31, 45, 50, 52, 60, 62, 64, 105, 111, 115, 116

# INDEX

LaPointe, Arthur  39
Lavigne, Victor  16
Le Pas  94
Lincoln, NH  34, 57
Littleton, NH  34, 37, 38
Lombard, Roland  51, 55, 58, 59, 68, 71, 73, 83
Lovejoy, Fred  15
Lowell, MA  34
Lyman Construction Company  62, 116
Lyman, Jim  60
Lyman, John H.  52, 59, 60, 68

# M

malamute  41, 42, 74, 80, 84, 87, 88, 89, 101, 105, 107, 108
Manchester  15, 34
Manitoba, Canada  33, 35, 38, 45, 63, 78, 94, 95
Marden, Bill Pynn  25, 26
Marqueis, Carmac  39
Martel, Emile  62
Mason, Hiram  16, 35, 36, 38
Massachusetts  15, 30, 31, 33, 34, 35, 43, 45, 82, 83
McDonald, William  33
McDougall, Malcolm  73
Mechanics Building  34
Meredith, NH  14, 16, 23, 24, 25, 30, 31, 33, 37, 39, 71, 81
Miner, Paula K.  19
Molburg, Cynthia  31, 52, 66, 81, 100, 111, 112
Molburg, Deborah  64, 68, 81, 82, 83, 113
Molburg, Dick  17, 49, 66, 69
Molley, Phillip  16
Moody, Ed  69, 70, 71
Moulton, Dick  25, 26, 50, 51, 67, 68, 71, 73, 81, 82, 83, 101
musher  20, 21, 23, 29, 31, 37, 41, 43, 45, 47, 58, 63, 64, 65, 66, 68, 73, 76, 77, 78, 82, 83, 96, 101, 103, 110, 111, 114

# N

Nashua, MA  34
New England Sled Dog Club  13, 14, 17, 21, 25, 26, 31, 32, 33, 34, 40, 41, 42, 45, 59, 64, 74, 79, 84, 93
Nome, Alaska  15, 38, 66, 76, 77, 92, 106, 112, 113, 114, 115
North American Classic  46
North Conway, NH  13, 16, 33, 34, 35, 36, 37
North Greenland Eskimo  106
North Woodstock  15, 25

# O

Olympics  29, 40, 41, 42, 84
open class  17, 27, 29, 45, 52
Ottawa, Canada  45, 62, 63, 73, 83

# P

Penacook  34
Peobody, Caryl  15
Piscopo, John  39
Plymouth, NH  34, 62
Plymouth State College  62
Poland Spring, ME  15, 31, 33, 35, 38, 73, 75
Prescott, Edgar B.  32

# Q

Quebec, Canada  13, 32, 33, 39, 41, 45, 50, 62, 63, 64, 68, 73, 106, 109, 111

# R

Read, Richard  15
Ricker, Almon  26
Ricker, Elizabeth M.  26, 38, 73
Roberts, Fred S.  32
Ropertz, Rudi  51
Rowe, C.E.  32
Russick, Shorty  13, 16, 33, 35, 36, 41, 42, 95
Rutter, Everett  14

# INDEX

## S

Samburgh, John  40
Samoyed  74, 103, 105, 106, 107
Sandwich, NH  30, 40, 55, 80
Seeley, Eva  42, 73, 74, 80, 83, 84, 87, 88
Seeley, Milton  16, 41, 73, 87
Seppala, Leonhard  15, 16, 31, 33, 36, 38, 39, 41, 42, 58, 63, 71, 72, 73, 74, 75, 76, 77, 78, 79, 92
Sevigny, Hector "Pete"  22
Shearer, William, III  16
Siberian husky  73, 74, 76, 84, 87, 102, 103, 107
Skeen, Henri  13, 16
Slocum, Lloyd  40
Souther, Harry  14, 33, 38
sprint  9, 29, 32, 45, 54, 64, 65, 66, 68, 99
St. Bernards  22, 31, 62, 64, 67, 82, 85, 91
Stearns, Richard  15
St. Godard, Emile  13, 16, 33, 36, 38, 39, 41, 42, 58, 63, 74, 78, 94, 95
Streeper, Eddy  40
Sylvain, Eddy  68

## T

Tamworth  30, 31, 35, 38, 78, 80, 91
Taylor, Moseley  33, 38, 41
*Team & Trail*  17, 31, 65, 69, 81, 82, 111
towline  99, 103
Town Team  23, 24, 25, 26, 31
Turmel, Real  40, 50
Twin Mountains  34

## V

Vaughan, Norman  16, 74
VFW  22, 23

## W

Walden, Arthur T.  13, 14, 16, 23, 31, 73, 78, 79, 80, 85, 86, 87, 88, 89, 91, 93, 96, 97

Weirs, The  39, 67
Wheeler, Harry  42
White, Dustin  14
White Mountain  11, 31, 32, 56, 57, 68, 114, 115
Wiggin, Alan  48
Winnipesaukee's Lakes Region  30, 33, 35, 39, 67
Winter Carnival  16, 23, 47, 60, 79, 87, 111
wolfhound  38, 95, 99
Wonalancet, NH  13, 14, 15, 30, 31, 40, 78, 80, 81, 85, 86, 87, 89, 91, 93
World Championship Sled Dog Derby  9, 14, 31, 39, 50, 60, 64, 68, 81, 83, 111, 115
World War II  16, 22, 57, 59, 72, 81

# ABOUT THE AUTHOR

Dr. Bruce Heald is a graduate of Boston University, the University of Massachusetts at Lowell and Columbia Pacific University. He is presently an adjunct professor of American history at Plymouth State University and a fellow in the International Biographical Association and the World Literary Academy in Cambridge, England. Dr. Heald is the recipient of the Gold Medal of Honor for literary achievement from the American Biographical Institute (1993). From 2005 to 2008, he was a state representative to the General Court of New Hampshire. He resides in Meredith, New Hampshire, with his family.

Dr. Heald has always loved the sport, and with enthusiasm, he wishes to preserve and write the history of dog sledding in New England.

Visit us at
www.historypress.net

www.ingramcontent.com/pod-product-compliance
Lightning Source LLC
Chambersburg PA
CBHW042144160426
43201CB00022B/2398